EQUALITY, EFFICIENCY, AND PROPERTY OWNERSHIP IN THE ISLAMIC ECONOMIC SYSTEM

Akhtar A. Awan

UNIVERSITY
PRESS OF
AMERICA

LANHAM • NEW YORK • LONDON

University Press of America,™ Inc.

4720 Boston Way
Lanham, MD 20706

3 Henrietta Street
London WC2E 8LU England

Printed in the United States of America

Library of Congress Cataloging in Publication Data

Awan, Akhtar A., 1949–
Equality, efficiency, and property ownership in the Islamic economic system.

Bibliography: p.
Includes indexes.
1. Economics—Religious aspects—Islam. I. Title.
BP173.75.A88 1983 330.15 83-16729
ISBN 0-8191-3562-3 (alk. paper)
ISBN 0-8191-3563-1 (pbk. : alk. paper)

All University Press of America books are produced on acid-free paper which exceeds the minimum standards set by the National Historical Publications and Records Commission.

Equality, Efficiency, and Property Ownership in the Islamic Economic System

To my father, Malik M. Yousaf Awan

Preface

The ideas on which this book is based were initially conceived at The Johns Hopkins University during the years 1978-1980. Later, in mid-March 1981, while advising the Libyan Ministry of Planning, I was invited by the Al-Fateh University to present views on "The Comparative Economic Systems." I used the occasion to bring together materials I had been developing over the past two years. This book emerged directly from the effort to respond to that invitation.

While the book is concerned with the Islamic economic system, the subject is treated with the standards of rigor of contemporary economists trained in the West. Some technical concepts and mathematical operations are employed for correct reasoning and for deeper understanding of the problems, but the concepts have also been given intuitive explanation for the non-technical reader.

My deep and lasting appreciation goes to all who have taught me, particularly Professor W. M. Gorman of Oxford University, Professor S. C. Salop of Georgetown Law School and Professor C. Y. Hsieh of The George Washington University. I have also benefited from discussions following my seminars at Al-Fateh University (Libya) and Caracas Central University (Venezuela). I am very grateful to Mehdi Imberesh, Mukhtar Dera, M. A. Farooqi, Sepala Weliwitigoda, Saleh Minina, Muhammad Shrief, Muhammad Farhat, Musa Abu Freiwa and Jenny Awan for their valuable suggestions and criticisms.

Akhtar A. Awan
Washington, D.C.
March 30, 1983

Contents

1

Economic Justice, Contemporary Economic Systems, and the Islamic Economy

"The most difficult issues of political economy are those where goals of efficiency, freedom of choice, and equality conflict. It is hard enough to propose an intellectually defensible compromise among them, even harder to find a politically viable compromise." Thus wrote Nobel laureate James Tobin in the beginning of his essay "On Limiting the Domain of Inequality," published in the *Journal of Law and Economics,* Vol. 13, October 1970. While the essay, alas, failed to provide any comprehensive solution which may have helped to achieve these goals of efficiency and equality simultaneously within the framework of the capitalist economic system, the issues posed in it did help me to reinforce my view about the Islamic economic system, a system which may resolve this important economic efficiency-equity trade-off phenomenon of our times.

The relation between the Islamic notion of dual ownership, which guarantees equal participation in the decision-making process of production and distribution, and economic justice is indeed a close one, and it turns both ways. It is clear that such participation is a common ingredient of social equality, but it is also important to note that participation in economic activities on the basis of equality depends substantially on possibilities of actual economic justice in society. The classical economists analyzing allocative efficiency and distributive justice did not find it particularly obnoxious to leave out distributive justice from allocative efficiency, and one reason why they could do it was because they could get away with it. But, as the quest of mankind for equality and justice has grown, it became clear that issues of allocation and distribution are closely intertwined and, thus, it also became far more important than ever to solve the allocation and distribution problems simultaneously.

In these essays, I am concerned with the Islamic economic system in a special context.[1] But I must argue that the historical nature of methodological aspects and the scope of capitalist and socialist economic systems are worth bearing in mind before going into the nature and operation of the Islamic economic system. Ultimately the relevance of our ideas on this subject must be judged by their ability to resolve the economic and social problems of our times.

1.1. The Historical Fallacy of Positive Economics

A general and yet unfortunate practice of modern economists is the use of dual labels to designate the same theory.[2] This is particularly true with the problem that concerns us here. The contention that positive economics has only to do with the capitalist economic system of the West is a historical fallacy; it is not correct. The socialist economic

[1] In particular, I shall be concerned primarily with equality, efficiency, and property ownership in the Islamic economic system.

[2] For instance, in probing the causes of economic depression, we often hear some economists laying the blame at the door of "underconsumption" while others cite "oversaving" as the villain. Actually, "oversaving" and "underconsumption," if properly defined, refer essentially to the same phenomenon.

system, as conceived by Marx and his followers, is also utterly a product of the positivist era of the West. This is not simply because its founders and leading figures are all Western, but rather socialism itself is the social cost of Industrial Revolution in the modern West. Marx, like other philosophers of the Nineteenth Century, saw in the Jacobian cult of reason an anticipation of positivism that replaces the metaphysical and theological era. The positivism in the Western perspective has been drawn into materialism, and it has undergone a similar fate in the capitalist and socialist economic systems. Given this a priori principle and method of perception, who could doubt that for the capitalist and socialist economic systems alike, the idea of progress and of production, the cult of materialism and of technology, are, and have been, the same.

The idea of progress is exactly the idea to suit a society eager to enjoy the material prosperity derived from technical progress. This idea has entered social consciousness through the writings of men like Abé de Saint-Pierre (1737) and the Marquis de Condorcet (1795) to become a dogma in the Nineteenth Century. Being a philosophy of change, the idea of progress calls for an ever-increasing mastery by man over his environment, mainly through the development of his knowledge and technology. It creates a confidence in the future and assures that tomorrow will be better than today. This hope for the future guarantees those whose present life is economically miserable that at least the future belongs to them. The future is the only kind of property the bourgeois capitalist willingly concedes to the workers, and the only kind of hope the socialist dictator willingly concedes to the laborers.

At any rate, both these divergent economic streams (capitalism and socialism) of today have their fountainhead in the cult of positivism. Classical liberalism and Marxism alike share, in theoryand practice, this positive economics. Both economic systems ultimately converge on a single view of material prosperity. The bourgeois tendencies of advanced communist societies which can no longer be simply dismissed—are no accident, no aberration, no revisionist deviation, because everything culminates in materialism, and it is only natural that those economic philosophies that are founded on materialism, no matter what their starting point, should finally enter upon the same road and have the same final destination.

1.2. **On the Boundaries of Positive Economic Systems**

The exponents of the capitalist market economy have usually assumed that since there is a single structure of economic theory, a single definition is feasible, and all other economies are unanalyzable or simply not very interesting. Robbins (1935) was quite clear on this point. "It has sometimes been asserted that the generalizations of economics are essentially historico-relative in character, that their validity is limited to certain historical conditions, and that outside these they have no relevance . . . . This view is a dangerous misapprehension . . . . It is only failure to realize this, and a too exclusive preoccupation with the subsidiary assumptions, which can lend any countenance to the view that the laws of economics are limited to certain conditions of time and space."[3] The Marxians, on the other hand, assert that "Bourgeois Economics" is a system of apologetics for capitalism. It has no relevance to a socialist economy.[4] Lange (1963) elaborates that "economic laws are not universally valid covering all stages of social development but are historical laws dealing with definite stages." Thus there is "the political economy of the primitive community . . . the political economy of feudalism, the political economy of capitalism, and the political economy of socialism. Each of these 'political economies' deals with the economic laws specific to its social formation, the mode of operation of that formation and its 'economic laws of move-

[3] L. Robbins, *An Essay on the Nature and Significance of Economic Science,* pp. 80-81.

[4] "Political economy is a science . . . of the unorganized national economy. Only in a society where production has an anarchistic character, do laws of social life appear as 'natural,' 'spontaneous' laws, independent of the will of individuals and groups, laws acting with the blind necessity of the law of gravity. Indeed, as soon as we deal with an organized national economy . . . the economy is regulated not by the blind forces of the market and competition, but by the consciously carried out plan . . . . The end of capitalist and commodity society signifies the end of political economy." Alec Nove, *The Soviet Economy:* An Introduction, p. 266.

ment' thereby providing an explanation of the process of emergence, development and decay of each social formation concerned."[5]

Differences on this issue are related to the boundaries of contemporary economic systems. The question whether Robbins' "universal economics" in terms of scarce means and competing ends or Lange's relative "political economy" is more generally valid, thus turns out to be complicated. To understand it completely, let us first highlight the distinctive features of both economic systems.

The capitalist economic system requires: (1) private ownership of, and private enterprise with, the means of production; (2) the predominance of economic gain as the guiding force in production decisions; and (3) reliance on markets and prices to allocate resources and distribute income. Whereas the socialist economy seeks to combine the socialist principles of (1) public ownership, and (2) comprehensive and detailed planning and control of almost all phases of economic life with (3) resources allocated primarily by administrative "commands" in real (physical) terms—such as production targets, allocation orders, etc.

The capitalist market economy clearly is based on the single principle of freedom (freedom is the rationale, but the system itself is defined, as above, in terms of ownership) that applies to the varied and tangled needs of society and possesses one and only one criterion—the criterion of maximization of wealth.[6] Thus, this particular kind of freedom of money making and profit-seeking which does not embody any logic of choice at random, constitutes the bedrock on which conventional market economic theory rests.[7] The socialist economic

[5] Oskar Lange, *Political Economy,* pp. 63, 94.

[6] "Maximization provides the moving force of economics. It asserts that any unit of the system will move toward an equilibrium position as a consequence of universal efforts to maximize utility or returns. Maximization is a general basic law that applies to the elementary units and, by the rules of composition, to larger and more complicated collections of those units." Sherman Roy Krupp, "Equilibrium Theory in Economics and in Functional Analysis as Types of Explanation," in *Functionalism in the Social Sciences,* p. 69.

[7] Koopmans, commenting on unsatisfying methodological efforts on

system, on the other hand, goes to the other extreme in that it insists on deliberate economic control of the means of production. The purpose here is the single principle of equality in material prosperity (equality in income and wealth is the purpose, but the system itself is defined, as we have described previously in terms of ownership). This system tends to usurp the individual's liberty of economic action; denies him the chance to exercise his initiative; and kills his work incentive. Now the situation becomes clearer. The capitalist economic system sought to restore the rights of individual ownership and assumed his freedom, and the socialist economy sought to release the laboring class from oppressive exploitation and believed in equality. As such, each sought to achieve social and economic justice. Yet each was a one-dimensional, unbalanced expression of social and economic justice and had tendencies toward monistic solutions. But, the richness and wisdom of life lie in pluralistic solutions and not in monistic solutions. A single pillar, no matter how strong and how thick, cannot support a multidimensional and multistory building. Similarly, a one-dimensional economic system based on a single-faceted ideology cannot solve multidimensional goals of efficiency, freedom of choice, and equality simultaneously.

1.3. The Paradox of Objective Economics and Value Judgement

If positive economic theory is born of a system of logic and lives in a kingdom where reason is to rule over morality, rather than be the mere servant of passion, then the policy recommendation that involves ethical judgement could never be made; if the task of a scientific theory such as positive economics is to merely develop explanatory statements about the operation of economy, then the contemporary economic systems would never attempt to evaluate their performances; and, if it is forbidden to say that social state x′ is preferred

---

the part of L. Robbins and M. Freedman, ends his essay with the lament: "One is led to conclude that economics as a scientific discipline is still somewhat hanging in the air." T. C. Koopmans, *Three Essays on the State of Economic Science,* p. 141.

to social state x, and since this implies precisely the distributional judgement, then Adam Smith would have never recommended increasing returns to scale and technical progress for faster economic growth, and Lenin in 1921 would never have insisted on distribution as a means of increasing production.

Indeed, Western economists and philosophers do not practice what they preach. Despite rhetorical statements in favor of positivism, they talk efficient allocation of resources and welfare economics based on certain value judgements. Welfare economics, whether pure or applied, obviously involves value judgements and there are good reasons to believe this. First, in welfare economics, prescriptions for policy are studied, and no prescription can ever be made without the notion of value judgement. Second, since any policy recommendation requires value judgements and welfare economics requires policy recommendations, any theorem incorporating welfare economics must rest on some implicit or explicit value judgements.

Although the idea of value-free "Scientific" welfare economics is simply a contradiction in terms, it is possible for welfare economists to pretend by adopting the argument that consensus on certain value judgements renders these judgements objective. This indeed has been the usual procedure in the literature of welfare economics. This is dangerous since such implicit value judgements lead to an essentially ideologically biased argument disguised as a scientific argument. In this context, it is perhaps worthwhile to review the literature of welfare economics and to expose the implicit value judgements in handling economic justice by the Western economists.

1.4. The Paretian Value Judgements

The new welfare economics is led by Pareto (1906), and followed by Bergson (1938), Samuelson (1950), and Graaff (1957). The central theorem of this new welfare economics states that the allocation of resources that is obtained in a competitive market equilibrium is Pareto-optimal, provided that (1) certain assumptions are met regarding nonnegativity, divisibility, the convexity of the tastes and technology, and the objectives of the decision-makers, and (2) the calculation of decision-makers takes into account the marginal effects of their actions on the utilities and/or costs of all affected economic agents. Since the purpose of this theorem is to allocate the resources optimally, it is necessarily based on the value judgements:

(i) Social state x′ is better than social state x if one or more individuals in the society prefer x′ to x and all other individuals are indifferent.
(ii) The individual should be considered the best judge of his own welfare.
(iii) Social welfare is to be considered a monotonic increasing function of individual welfare.

Let us explore the validity of these value judgements with respect to economic justice. Assume that there are only two individuals named Mr. A and Mr. B and two allocations named x and x′ are under consideration. By associating with each allocation its utility possibility set, we have

$$U = \{u^A(z^A), u^B(z^B): z^A + z^B = x^A + x^B\} \quad (1)$$

and

$$U' = \{u^A(z^A), u^B(z^B): z^A + z^B = x'^A + x'^B\} \quad (2)$$

The upper right-hand boundary of this set is called the utility possibility frontier. The utility possibility frontier gives the utility distributions associated with all Pareto-efficient reallocations of x and x′. To see this, consider Figure 1.1. Notice that any change from initial allocation x to new allocation x′ on the utility possibility frontier will not make Mr. A indifferent. As a matter of fact, the Paretian criterion falls to the ground as Mr. A suffers a diminished sense of well-being as a result of gain experienced by the better off Mr. B. This precisely implies that initially poor Mr. B cannot be made any better off without cutting into the affluence of the rich Mr. A; the situation would still be Pareto-optimal despite the disparity between Mr. A and Mr. B.

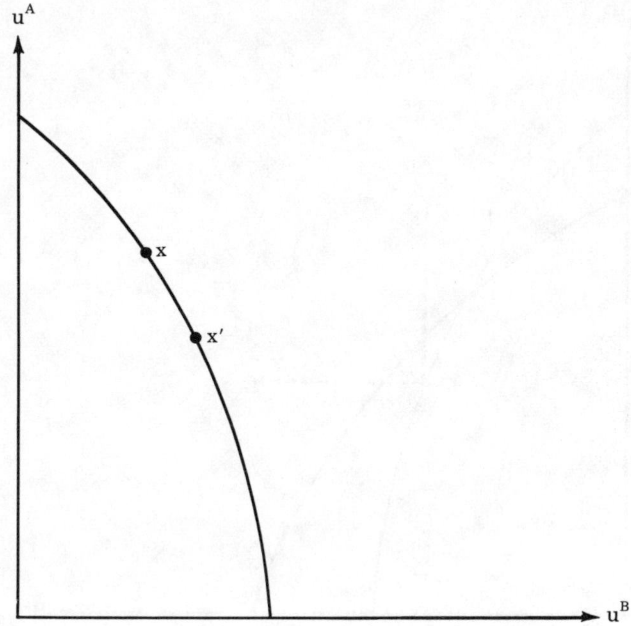

Figure 1.1

Another ideologically biased value judgement of this new welfare economics is that the individual is the best judge of his own welfare. But compulsory education, compulsory national insurance, taxes on tobacco and alcohol, subsidized farm products, libraries, and national parks are only a few obvious examples based on the value judgement that in some matters an individual is not the best judge of his own welfare.

Last, but by no means least, the third value judgement of this new welfare economics is that social welfare is to be considered a monotonic increasing function of individual welfare, that if one individual's income increases while those of others remain the same, then social welfare increases. If 100 pound half-starved Mr. B makes a mutually beneficial agreement with 300 pound fat Mr. A to carry him on his shoulders across the river, and no one in society cares, there has been a Paretian improvement in social welfare. This situation is il-

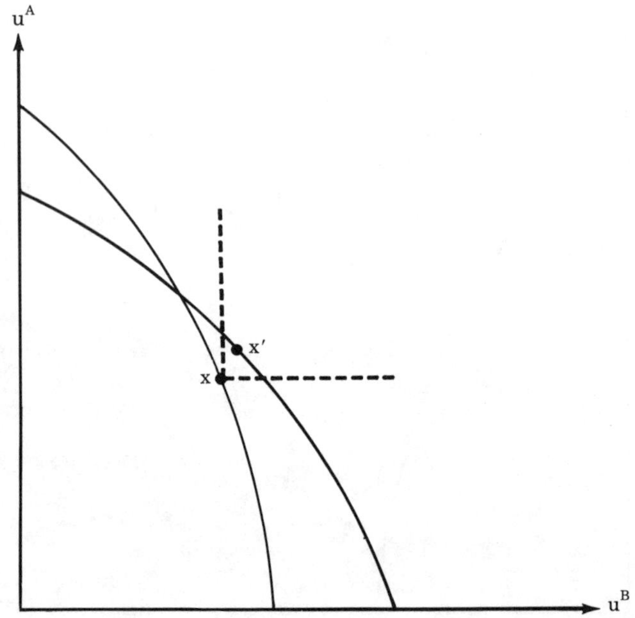

Figure 1.2

lustrated in Figure 1.2. Notice that the mutually beneficial agreement between Mr. A and Mr. B does help half-starved Mr. B, but enriches fat Mr. A much more. This essentially implies that such a value judgement generates an unfavorable relative distribution of income and wealth and increases the gap between the rich and the poor. Since the only issue in this problem is that of distribution, the Paretian value judgements have no power to restore economic justice. Thus, an additional criterion is needed to identify the "just" point from among the many Pareto-optimal points on the utility possibility frontier.

1.5. Additional Criteria for Social Choice

Robbins (1935) argued that economists as scientists can endorse only those policies that produce a Pareto improvement that makes some individuals better off and makes no one worse off. Following Robbins, Harrod (1936) immediately jumped to the conclusion that the repeal of the Corn Laws in 1846 was not based on the Pareto principle. Although it increased the real income of consumers in Britain by more than it decreased the real income of British landlords, it did not prove that the repeal constituted an actual Pareto improvement, i.e., an economic benefit to some and no worsening for anyone.

In response, Kaldor (1939) and Hicks (1939) proposed "The Compensation Criterion." Kaldor argued that if as a result of some policy change some people are made economically better off while some others are made worse off than before, it might still be possible for the economist to make a value-free recommendation of the policy, provided the gainers can compensate the losers so that the losers will accept the change; after the compensation payments are made, the gainers are better off and the losers are none the worse off. Since the compensation need not actually be paid, a Kaldor improvement offers only a potential Pareto improvement. Note that application of the Kaldor criterion using market prices requires each of the Paretian value judgements mentioned in section 1.4. In other words, Kaldor proposed that the new social state x′ be considered an improvement over the old social state x, if, under that new policy, there would be possible a set of redistributive income transfers that could produce some social state x″, that would be Pareto-superior to the old state x. Kaldor, however, gave no explanation for methods of income transfer under the new policy.

In any case, Scitovsky (1941) demonstrated that the Kaldor criterion can yield a paradoxical result, i.e., a move from the old social state x to the new social state x′ is an improvement, and so is a move from the new social state x′ to the old social state x. Let us state this paradoxical result a bit more formally: in Figure 1.3, x′ is preferred to x, since x″ is Pareto-preferable to x; but then x is also preferred to x′ since x‴ is preferred to x′.

Moreover, Scitovsky proposed the double criterion for an improvement in welfare. He argued that (1) a move from social state x to social state x″ is an improvement on the Hicks-Kaldor criterion and (2) that the return move from social state

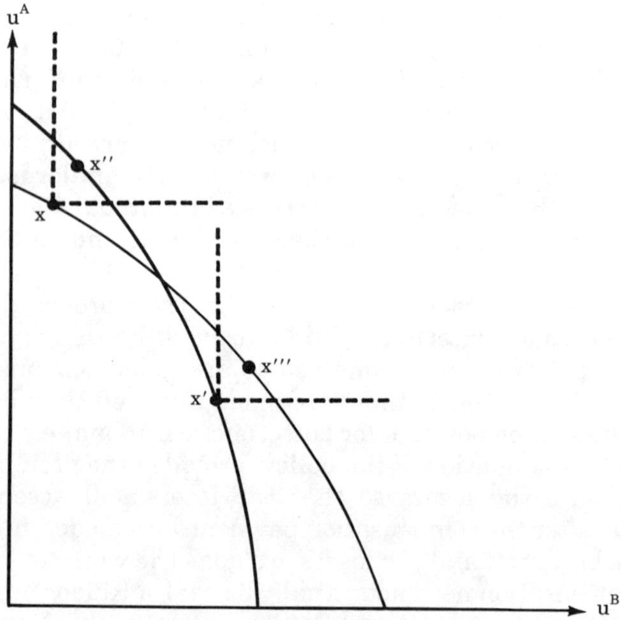

Figure 1.3

x'' to social state x is not an improvement on the Hicks-Kaldor criterion. This is clearly another burden that has befallen economic justice in the name of value-free economic welfare. Since Scitovsky's double criterion recommends a move from social state x to social state x'' rather than x' or x''' in Figure 1.3, the disparity between rich Mr. A and poor Mr. B will increase continuously.

Samuelson (1950) pointed out that a change in social state will be an unambiguously potential improvement if, and only if, a new utility possibility frontier lies everywhere outside the old one; in other words, potential superiority of x''' (in Figure 1.4) to x requires that for every distribution of x, there should be a distribution of x''' in which at least one person is better off and no one is worse off. But such a result is possible only when the utility possibility frontier is drawn on the assumption of lump-sum redistribution. Thus, Western

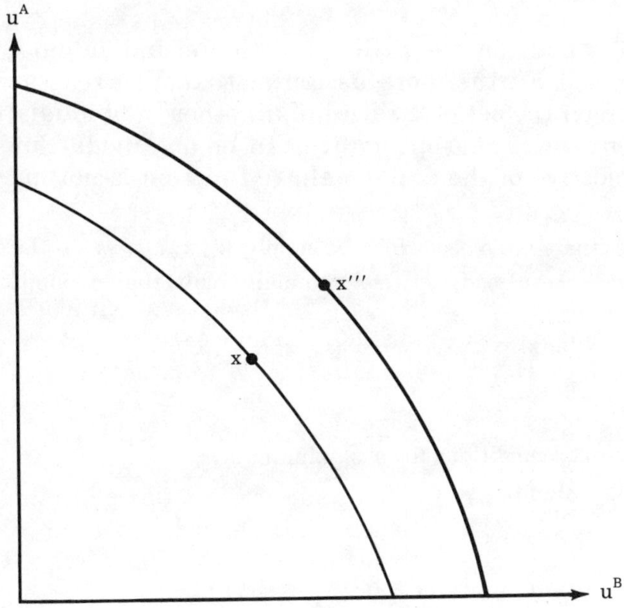

Figure 1.4

economists need some new economic and social system to bring about the uniform shift of the utility possibility frontier which will produce an actual Pareto improvement in everyone's lot.

1.6. The Bergson Social Welfare Function and Arrow's Theorem

The motivation of modern economists to invent some scientific tools for distributional judgement beyond Pareto-optimality involves the most important task of the last four decades. Bergson's (1938) invention of the social welfare function is the main result of such motivation. The essential feature of the Bergson social welfare function is that it is individualistic and purely ordinal in the sense that it can be expressed as

$$\max W = W[u^1(x^1), u^2(x^2), \ldots, u^m(x^m)] \qquad (3)$$

Here, u^1 stands for the utility function of individual i, for $i = 1, \ldots, m$. Furthermore, assuming that W increases with any u^i given the set of utilities of all other individuals, the conditions for Pareto-optimality can be obtained.[8] But the main objective of the social welfare function is not merely

[8]Suppose there are n goods in fixed supply: $x_1, x_2, \ldots, x_n$. If the goal is to allocate these goods between two individuals, then maximize W:

$$\max W = W[u^1(x_1^1, x_2^1, \ldots, x_n^1), u^2(x_1^2, x_2^2, \ldots, x_n^2)]$$

The first order conditions for a maximum are:

$$\frac{\partial W}{\partial x_1^1} = \frac{\partial W}{\partial x_1^2}$$

$$\frac{\partial W}{\partial x_2^1} = \frac{\partial W}{\partial x_2^2}$$

$$\vdots \qquad \vdots$$

$$\frac{\partial W}{\partial x_n^1} = \frac{\partial W}{\partial x_n^2}$$

where,

$$\frac{\partial W}{\partial x_1^1} = \frac{\partial W}{\partial u^1} \cdot \frac{\partial u^1}{\partial x_1^1}$$

and

$$\frac{\partial W}{\partial x_1^2} = \frac{\partial W}{\partial u^2} \cdot \frac{\partial u^2}{\partial x_1^2}$$

to construct a Pareto-optimal point, but also to go a step forward beyond this extremely limited concept by arriving at the "just" point or at least a ranking of different social states.

Arrow in the early 1950's was first to pose the question whether there exist general conditions which can be imposed on the relation between the set of individual preferences and the ranking of different social states. Arrow proved that if it was desired to have, for each logically possible configuration of individual preferences over the feasible social states, a social ranking of these states that satisfied three seemingly unobjectionable logical conditions (transitivity, unrestricted domain, and independence of irrelevant alternatives) it would have to violate either of the two seemingly unobjectionable ethical conditions (The Pareto Principle and Nondictatorship). Arrow's proof cannot be appreciated fully without consider-

---

This is true for all other derivatives. Rewriting the first-order conditions as:

$$\frac{\partial W}{\partial u^1} \cdot \frac{\partial u^1}{\partial x_1^1} = \frac{\partial W}{\partial u^2} \cdot \frac{\partial u^2}{\partial x_1^2}$$

$$\frac{\partial W}{\partial u^1} \cdot \frac{\partial u^1}{\partial x_2^1} = \frac{\partial W}{\partial u^2} \cdot \frac{\partial u^2}{\partial x_2^2}$$

And dividing one by the other gives:

$$\frac{\dfrac{\partial u^1}{\partial x_1^1}}{\dfrac{\partial u^1}{\partial x_2^1}} = \frac{\dfrac{\partial u^2}{\partial x_1^2}}{\dfrac{\partial u^2}{\partial x_2^2}}$$

i.e., the MRS between x_1 and x_2 must be equal for two individuals. These are precisely the necessary conditions for Paretian-optimality in exchange.

ing his conditions; though it is a bit tedious, his conditions are expressed below:

1. *Transitivity:* The ranking must be transitive. For all x, x′, and x″ in X, if $x > x'$, $x' > x''$, then $x > x''$.
2. *Unrestricted domain:* All logically possible sets of preferences can be included.
3. *Independence of irrelevant alternatives:* If new social states become feasible, this fact should not affect the social ranking of the original states; i.e., for any pair x, x′, if $x > x'$, then this will remain true if some new state x‴ becomes feasible.
4. *Pareto Principle:* For any pair x, x′, if everyone finds $x \geqslant x'$ (bundle x is at least as good as the bundle x′) and someone finds $x > x'$ (bundle x is strictly better than the bundle x′), then x is preferable.
5. *Nondictatorship:* One person's preferences should not determine society's preferences.

Arrow showed that these conditions are not compatible with one another and thus no general social relationship satisfying conditions 1-5 exists. Symbolically, assume there are three social states (x, x′, and x″) and two individuals (Mr. A and Mr. B). Suppose individuals are asked to rank social states by giving them a number from 1 to 3; the largest number for an outcome implies that it is the most preferred and so on. Furthermore, assume we get the following data:

	Social States		
Individuals	x	x′	x″
Mr. A	3	2	1
Mr. B	2	1	3

Now, using the tastes of Mr. A and Mr. B among x, x′, and x″, we can see the kind of inconsistencies which can arise in social choice. Since Mr. A prefers x′ to x″ and Mr. B prefers x″ to x′, it must be the case that society is indifferent between x′ and x″. Otherwise, society's preferences would be in accord with only one individual and this would violate the nondictatorship condition. Furthermore, since both individuals prefer x to x′, conditions 2, 3, and 4 require that $x > x'$. Hence, by condition 1, $x > x''$. But, again this is a violation of condition 5, since x″ is preferred to x by Mr. B.

Thus, it must be clear that if one were to specify the weights in the Bergson welfare function, one would obtain from it a ranking of different social states according to their social welfares. But, Arrow seems to have shown that such an exact social welfare function cannot generally be constructed without violating the ethical conditions.

A great deal of controversy has arisen over Arrow's impossibility theorem during the last thirty years. We do not intend here to go into the controversy over the formal validity of the theorem. Instead, we wish to discuss the most relevant objections that concern us here regarding the distributional judgements. It is to be noted that Arrow's theorem is true only if none of his conditions are to be violated. But, the desirability of his third condition has scant appeal in the real world. This condition simply implies the ranking of two social states and completely ignores the intensity with which each individual prefers one state to another. If the intensity of preferences is considered relevant in determining the welfare criteria, then we have to employ a system of weighing the individual preferences or utilities. This is a matter of interpersonal comparison of utilities and beyond any doubt such comparison requires value judgements. And, since value judgements are required for welfare criteria and for policy recommendation, there is no reason why we should not include interpersonal comparison of utility as ethical comparisons in our analysis.

Furthermore, the nondictatorship postulate seems highly unacceptable when considered in the context of Arrow's other conditions. This can be clearly seen by going into Arrow's exercise. Mr. B who prefers x″ to x to x′ receives no more weight than Mr. A who prefers x to x′ to x″. Everyone in the society would agree in this case that all of these social states leave Mr. B miserable compared to Mr. A. Thus, there is no room in the Arrowian welfare function for favoring the poor over the rich. In other words, economic justice is completely eliminated in such types of welfare economics.

1.7. The Moral Arithmetic of Utilitarians

It is often remembered that utilitarians used their notion of a "moral arithmetic" to justify a wide range of government activities in the economy, including redistributive activities. But, it is often forgotten that their peculiar notion of "moral arithmetic" blended with psychological and economical hedonism (the view that all actions are motivated by the desire to achieve pleasure and avoid pain) was not meant to help the poor, but rather to enrich the top class much more. Bentham (1789), whose utilitarianism[9] provided the initial impetus to utility theory, believed that maximizing the happiness "on the whole" would generally maximize everyone's happiness. Therefore, the sum of individual utilities should be taken as the measure of social welfare. Thus, according to him

$$W = u^A + u^B \qquad (4)$$

and

$$\Delta W = \Delta u^A + \Delta u^B \qquad (5)$$

In Bentham's and other classical utilitarians' view, social welfare increases if a simple sum of utilities increases. Utilitarian moral philosophy is concerned with the bigger sum and highly unconcerned with the interpersonal distribution of this sum. In their scheme, a loss of the poor Mr. B's utility is no loss of social welfare if just offset by an increment in the rich Mr. A's utility of the same magnitude. No doubt the entire notion is severely limited and supremely unsuitable for economic justice.

Interestingly enough, as the "marginal revolution"[10] took place in microstatic analysis in the early 1870's, utilitarianism developed the reputation of being an egalitarian criterion. Marshall noted that given total income and some

[9]Utilitarianism is led by Bentham (1789) and followed by Marshall (1890), Pigou (1920), Lange (1942), Robertson (1952), Lerner (1944), and Tinbergen (1970), etc.

[10]The marginal revolution is taken to refer to the discovery of the principle of diminishing marginal utility as a foundation of microeconomic analysis by Jevons, Menger, and Walras.

utility function for everyone, maximization of the sum of individual utilities between different persons requires equating the marginal utilities from income of different persons. This, in fact, amounts to equating total utilities. To see, consider two individuals Mr. A and Mr. B and one good x^0 that can be distributed between Mr. A and Mr. B. If both individuals have the same utility function and marginal utility of income diminishes with income, then the problem can be expressed as

$$\max W = u(x^A) + u(x^0 - x^A) \tag{6}$$

Where,

$$u' > 0 \text{ and } u'' < 0$$

The solution is

$$u'(x^A) = u'(x^B) \rightarrow x^A = x^B \tag{7}$$

But, this argument in support of equality falls to the ground when we go into the true character of the utilitarians' approach by considering a case where Mr. B is a cripple and derives exactly half the utility Mr. A would get from the same income x. In other words, this simply implies that the person making the judgement regards Mr. A's position as being twice as good as Mr. B's position for any given level of income. Symbolically, if

$$u^A = u(x^A) \tag{8}$$

then

$$u^B = \tfrac{1}{2}u(x^B) \tag{9}$$

In this case, the rule of maximizing the sum of total utility requires

$$\max W = u(x^A) + \tfrac{1}{2}u(x^0 - x^A) \tag{10}$$

Figure 1.5 based on Sen (1973) illustrates the solution.[11] The

[11]A. K. Sen, *On Economic Inequality,* p. 17.

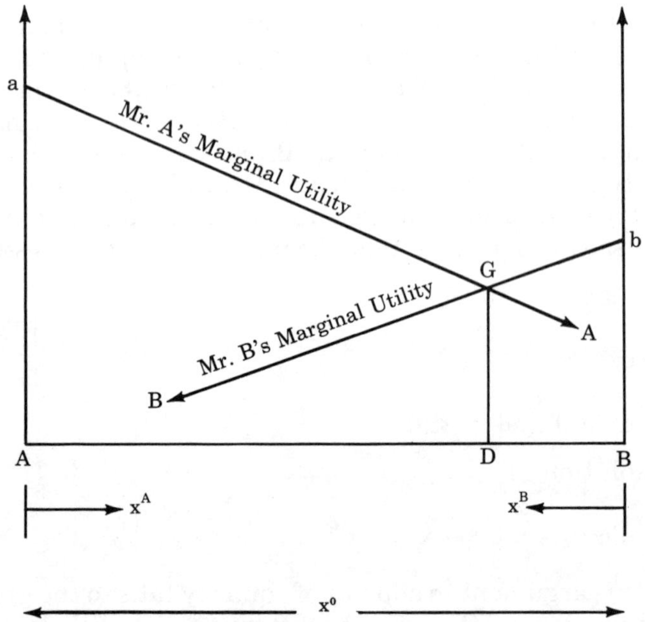

Figure 1.5

optimal point is D with Mr. A enjoying a total utility of AaGD and Mr. B only BbGD.

Thus, instead of reducing the inequality between healthy Mr. A and crippled Mr. B, the utilitarian approach of distribution compounds it by giving more income to an already rich Mr. A. It is, therefore, absurd to even think that utilitarianism is an egalitarianism.[12]

[12]The leading modern day alternative to utilitarianism is provided by J. Rawls (*A Theory of Justice*, 1971). Rawls argues that participation in society is akin to participation in a game of chance with respect to assets that largely determine a way of life and therefore of happiness. Since the existing distribution of assets may well be unfair, inquiries on the nature of just institution cannot depend on any particular outcome of this game. Therefore, individuals must step behind a veil of ignorance and decide on a contract as if they were uncertain of their actual position in the society. When this is done, two principles emerge:

1.8. **Marxian Distributive Justice**

Many economists, contemplating social and economic contrasts between the socialist and capitalist societies, account the former different from the latter from the standpoint of economic justice. But we clearly see that socialist economies, although they have attained a relatively better distribution of income and wealth, closely resemble the capitalist economies with respect to the principle of production, the value of the tools of production, the principle of material abundance, the division of labor, and, in particular, the theory and practice of economic justice.

By annexing "dialectical" to "materialism," Marx and Marxians not only withhold "basic" ethical postulates, but also set up a materialistic determinism over and above them, which at the level of practical application, amounts to another chain. For this truly leads to the fettering of social choice and ultimately plunges social and economic justice into the same pit of mathematical determinism that upholders of capitalist economics have dug for it.

"Material abundance" is proclaimed the essential prerequisite for realizing the ideal communal economies; and the prerequisite for this abundance, in turn, is the transformation of society into a massively industrialized system. This transformation is based on the principles derived from capitalism—that is to say, specialization, a typical techno-bureaucratic institutional framework, and competition based upon individual self-interest. Beyond all this, there is a single organization working rapidly to embrace all members of society

---

(1) each person is to have an equal right to the most extensive basic liberty compatible with a similar liberty for others; (2) social and economic inequalities are to be arranged so that they are both (a) to the greatest benefit of the least advantaged and (b) attached to offices and positions open to all under conditions of fair equality of opportunity.

This is equivalent to maximization of minimum welfare. The objection to the Rawlsian maximin rules is their extreme nature, concentrating only on the worst off individual and ignoring the rest. The main motive behind the theory is not to eliminate inequality between the rich and the poor, but to preserve the self-interest of the rich and to establish a charitable capitalist state in a contractarian fashion.

and, over it, a new class of rulers consisting of the leading bureaucrats—likewise capitalists.

Thus, once again we find state capitalism in the name of socialism; governmental dictatorship in the name of "dictatorship of the proletariat," and an axiomatic, rather than ethical, principle of mechanism and economicism for the sake of quickly attaining economic abundance.

To show a bit more systematically, let us present a proposition within the framework of Marxian analysis which rules out economic justice in a society. Note that the objective of presenting this proposition is to clarify a basic weakness of the Marxian approach in handling problems of distribution and equality.

The Marxian Condition. Society is divided into two parts, infrastructure and superstructure. Infrastructure can be called "mode of production," which is determined in accordance with the nature of the "means of production." The form of the superstructure—which comprises ethical, political, social, economic, and so forth, to every shade of ideology—then arises from the "means of production."

Proposition 1.1.

The only economy satisfying the Marxian condition must rule out economic justice.

Proof Assume not. Then infrastructure of capitalist and socialist economies is different. But we know that Marxian infrastructure is derived from the "means of production" that include tools, factories, equipments, production skills and knowledge of the labor force, natural resources, and the general level of technology. Besides, these "means of production" and the notion of the absolute ownership (private or public) of these "means of production" in capitalist and socialist economies are the same. Thus, if superstructure arises from these "means of production" and absolute ownership of these "means of production," then economic justice can also be achieved in a capitalist economy which contradicts the Marxian repudiation of capitalism.

1.9. Economic Justice and the Islamic Economy

Given Marxian belief in dialectical materialism and that labor is entitled, as a kind of right, to the full product of its toil, the injustice of capitalism, in which capital may be privately owned and the owner may take a share of product, it is clear that the system is purely axiomatic, rather than a result deduced from more basic ethical postulates.[13] Since there is no such thing as economic justice without ethical postulates, we are back to a situation where judgements on economic justice are not permitted.

Where lies the flaw? We would argue that the real trouble lies not only in the non-ethical behavior in handling economic justice, but also in the very foundations of contemporary economic systems which make economic justice dependent on the notion of absolute ownership. The ownership rights in both capitalism and socialism are defined in absolute terms such that either an individual owns the property in the absolute sense or the state owns the property in the absolute sense. Note that even in hybrid or mixed situations, where the tenure is by both private individual and public sector, the notion of ownership remains absolute. Implicit in the notion of such ownership is the idea that is founded on the Hobbesian argument of egoism.[14] There is no concept of dual ownership in these systems such that everyone is merely a "trustee" and "beneficiary" of ownership and yet no one owns in the traditional sense.[15] And this is precisely what makes these systems so remarkably unsuited to the analysis of distributional questions.

The crucial question really concerns dual ownership, since

[13]W. A. Wood, for example, in his "The Marxian Critique of Justice," *Philosophy and Public Affairs,* 1 (1972), pp. 244-282, says that there is nothing problematic about saying that disguised exploitation, unnecessary servitude, economic instability, and declining productivity (features that Marx argued capitalism possessed) are features of a productive system that constitute good reasons for condemning it. All the disputes that we have with Marx are over his economics and sociology.

[14]See T. Hobbes, *Leviathan* (reprinted in Melden), pp. 192-205.

[15]Strictly, this type of dual ownership is called "weak dual ownership," "strong dual ownership" requires the economic framework prescribed in Islam that will be discussed later in this section.

ethical postulates alone—it is easy to check—will not help us much. With ethical postulates we can primarily rely on income transfer (the dominant tradition of Marxian and capitalist economists for income distribution), rather than a comprehensive system that offers dual ownership which, we argue, is the case for economic justice. Although any transference of income from a relatively rich man to a relatively poor man of similar temperament may increase the level of satisfaction of a poor man, yet "it is at best a necessary but not a sufficient condition" for achieving economic justice.[16] Thus, it seems reasonable to argue that if the normative approach is to give any substantial help for economic justice, then the approach must be broadened to include the concept of dual ownership in the analysis. The question may be asked at this stage whether or not the concept of dual ownership is at all legitimate, and if so, in what sense. But, before we define dual ownership in a precise manner, it is, I think, fair to see the rationale behind the notion of absolute ownership in historical perspectives.

The concept of dual ownership, which includes general welfare and common good for the society, is perhaps as old as the beginning of the communal system in ancient history. However, it lost its sacrosanct aura as early as 1714 when Bernard Mandeville published *The Fable of the Bees: Or Private Vices, Publick Benefits,* in which he put forth the seemingly strange paradox that the vices most despised in the older moral code, if practiced by all, would result in the greatest public good. Selfishness, greed, and acquisitive behavior, he maintained, all tend to contribute to an industrious and thriving economy. The answer to the paradox was, of course, that what had been vices in the eyes of the medieval moralists were the very motivational forces that propelled the new capitalist system. And in view of the new moral and economic philosophies of capitalism, during the period of Industrial Revolution, these motives were no longer vices. It was during this period of industrialization that the individualistic ownership view of classical liberalism became the dominant

[16]Sen, *On Economic Inequality,* pp. 18-20.

ideology of capitalism.[17] The psychological, political, and economic creed of classical liberalism led pre-Marx socialists and Karl Marx himself to believe that individualistic ownership was the source of the inequalities and exploitation that existed in the capitalist economy.[18]

They argued that the presence of inequality essentially meant the presence of economic injustice and that capitalist commerce existed "for the purpose of pumping the sweat and blood of more or less everybody in order to form lakes of gold for the benefit of the few."[19] These economic injustices caused by individualistic ownership, Marx believed, would lead to the overthrow of capitalism and its replacement by a socialist society. But, Marx could not conceive clearly that if the ownership is defined in an absolute sense, as in capitalism in which selfishness, greed, and acquisitive behavior are inserted in a concealed or implicit way, then individualistic ownership or public ownership will not make much difference. When all ownership of capital is in the hands of the proletariat state and the proletariat state is set up as hierarchy, it becomes established and evolves into a bureaucracy; the proletariat state thus takes the form of a self-perpetuating

[17]This account of classical liberalism relies heavily on Harry K. Girvetz, *The Evolution of Liberalism,* pp. 1-149.

[18]Classical liberalism's psychological creed was based on four assumptions about human nature. People were believed to be egoistic, coldly calculating, essentially inert, and atomistic. The egoism argued by Hobbes furnished the basis of this view, and in the work of later liberals, especially Jeremy Bentham, it was blended with psychological hedonism: the idea that all actions are motivated by the desire to achieve pleasure and avoid pain.

The political creed of classical liberalism was to reject state or government. They believed government as an evil to be tolerated only when it was the sole means of avoiding a worse evil.

The economic benefits of division of labor were the foundation stone of the economic creed of classical liberalism. Note that Adam Smith's analysis of the market as an "invisible hand" that channeled egoistic drives into the most socially useful activities supported this doctrine of Laissez-faire. The only functions this philosophy assigned to the government were those that would support and encourage profit-making activities.

[19]Alexander Gray, *The Socialist Tradition,* p. 105.

ruling clique with selfish, ruthless, and greedy behavior. In such a system, all other persons will be merely employees and a similar relation will emerge as in capitalism. It is then clear that when a ruling hierarchy makes decisions for the people and determines production and consumption, it takes away economic justice.

It seems fairly clear that the rationale behind absolute ownership is very far from the egalitarian and ethical considerations that could lead to social and economic justice in a society. It is, therefore, odd that virtually all attempts for economic justice (by Marx and Marxian economists) or exercises in deriving optimal distributional rules (by capitalist economists) have been based on absolute ownership.

Finally, we come to the point where we can bring in egalitarian considerations into the notion of ownership. The framework which we pursue here, in particular, is the economic framework prescribed in Islam. According to this framework, the real ownership of wealth, consumable or productive, belongs to God. Man's temporal possession is limited and granted by God; man is merely a "trustee" for a term. Realization of this dual ownership mitigates against selfish and dishonest tendencies that often result from the deceitful notion of absolute ownership. It is interesting to observe that implicit in the notion of "trusteeship" and testing through wealth and worldly success is the idea that material superiority does not entail higher merit. Righteousness is the only criterion that raises the rank of a person with God.[20]

It might be thought that dual ownership cannot be practiced without the institution of Islamic framework. But this is not quite the case. Although the Islamic institution, of course, is a strong condition for such ownership, it is possible to visualize a weak condition for dual ownership without bringing the conceptual idea of God into analysis, and that is, where everyone is merely a "trustee" and a "beneficiary" of ownership and no one owns in a traditional sense. Whatever the line of argument one wishes to pursue for dual ownership, one is essentially asking for the radical overhaul of basic institutions.

[20]Qur'ān 49: 13.

Once the economic system has been broadened to include the concept of dual ownership, a comprehensive method for economic justice becomes available. Since by definition of dual ownership everyone is merely a "trustee" and a "beneficiary" of ownership and no one owns in a traditional sense, then there is no reason why some should be assigned a larger share and others should be assigned a smaller share of a fixed pie. It seems fairly clear that dual ownership lays its foundations on the idea of community in which everyone is a partner in the economic process of production and distribution. Unlike the utilitarian and the Marxian approaches, in which either maximizing the sum of individual utilities is taken as the measure of social welfare or a planning authority determines the level of social welfare, the Islamic economic approach seems to demand not only relative gains and losses of everyone, but also insists on full participation by everyone in determining the level of social welfare. To see how economic justice can be achieved in the Islamic economy, we propose the following axiom.

The Economic Justice Axiom. Let different individuals be endowed with different amounts of ability to produce the same good. Then following the even division of fixed initial bundle $\overline{W}$ among n individuals, distribution of any additional income generated by such an economy according to each person's contribution will lead to economic justice.

Two qualifications for the Economic Justice Axiom (EJA) should be specified here. First, the normative appeal of EJA would likely depend on the precise interpretation of the Islamic economy. In the Islamic economic framework, dual ownership guarantees equality in ownership and thus equal distribution of initial wealth $\overline{W}$ among all individuals in a given community. This equal distribution of initial wealth in the Islamic economy requires not only symmetry "from the outside" which is possible simply by dividing the initial bundle $\overline{W}$ equally, but also internal symmetry in the sense that an allocation x is equitable if no one prefers the bundle of any other individual to his own.

Second, EJA seems to demand harmony between ethical postulates and rational rules in the Islamic economy. It is ethical when we divide the initial bundle $\overline{W}$ evenly, but it is logical when we compare consumption-output bundles.

After the fair distribution of initial wealth, if I envy another person, I am saying that not only do I prefer to consume what he is consuming, but I also would be willing to produce what he is producing. However, these disparities in consumption are subject to certain constraints under the operation of social institution. Note that in such an economy, neither the "able" are being exploited by the "unable," nor are the "unable" being exploited by the "able." It simply provides economic justice for everyone.

1.10. Conclusions and Summary

We have noted that contemporary economic systems lay their foundations in the cult of positivism which makes these systems so remarkably unsuited to handling economic justice. The Pareto-optimality (including the basic theorem of welfare economics) does not provide a unique solution even if the Paretian value judgements are accepted. The compensation criterion and double criterion for an improvement of social welfare do not seem to help very much either. The standard approach of the social welfare function, because of its concentration on individual ordering only, fails to provide a framework for distributional discussions. The moral arithmetic of the utilitarians which has developed the reputation of being an egalitarian criterion is, in fact, capable of producing strongly anti-egalitarian results. Marxian dialectical materialism, on the other hand, as an approach to economic justice, cannot take us very far. This is brought out rather dramatically in Proposition 1.1. Finally, we have shown that social distributive judgements can be meaningfully expressed in terms of dual ownership within the framework of the Islamic economic system. Thus, the future for economic justice is not as bleak in the Islamic economic system as it seems under contemporary economic systems.

2

On the Economic Theory of Islam

In order to discuss the method of allocating resources in the Islamic economy, we must start our discussion by explaining, far more carefully than we were able to do in the preceding chapter, what kind of Islamic economy we have in mind. This matter is not a simple one because there exists no such economy in the real world at the present time, and hence, it is difficult to identify such an economy on the grounds of the economic framework prescribed in Islam. To say that the Islamic economy is exactly the type of economy we find today in Saudi Arabia, Libya, or Iran would be as incorrect and one-sided as to say that the dual ownership framework consists of a number of abstract principles derived from the real experience or the actual performance of the present Islamic world.

Fortunately, there is historical evidence which will help

us in seeking a definition. In the early days of Islam such an economy existed in the Islamic world and it performed perfectly. It is possible to derive a large number of characteristics of such an Islamic economy. However, a very large number of characteristics may be termed non-essential due to sociological differences among Muslim countries. But, they can still be adjusted to the particular situation or circumstances in a particular country. Indeed, this flexibility might be highly desirable if a specific Islamic economy were designed for, say, Pakistan in Asia or Libya in Africa. We thus have to concentrate here only on what we may term essential characteristics of the Islamic economic system; the rest can be left for adaptation to specific conditions. In fact, it is this adaptability that makes—or at least promises to make—the Islamic economy universally appealing.

2.1. The Characteristics of an Islamic Economy

The Islamic economy that concerns us is defined by three essential characteristics. These characteristics help us to possess all the relevant information regarding the knowledge of property rights structure and the system of preferences, which, I believe, are essential to construct an Islamic economic order.

(i) *Dual Ownership.* The Islamic economy is composed of a large number of small firms. The property rights structure of the "representative"[1] firm is based upon the concept of dual ownership. As we have mentioned earlier, dual ownership is a unique notion which completely differs from the traditional sense of ownership. Although it fully acknowledges the right of private ownership of the means of production, yet an owner should be aware of the fact that, in the last analysis, all wealth, including land, is truly owned by God and Man is merely a "trustee" and "beneficiary" of this ownership. Thereby, it establishes two points: that of acknowledging God as the sole creator and the owner of the uni-

[1]To forge a link between the behavior of firms and the state of the Islamic economy, it is convenient to adopt the fiction of the representative firm. It is also assumed that all firms in the Islamic economy are "representative."

verse, and that of equalizing all men in their spiritual and economic pursuits as creatures of God.[2]

Given this notion of dual ownership, the question can be asked how much this type of property rights structure actually helps us to develop a satisfactory theory of an Islamic economy? The precise answer to this question is, of course, our ultimate aim and will be discussed in the later part of this chapter when we explain how an Islamic economy actually works. However, we may attempt here a brief explanation. We understand that a firm in an Islamic economy can be created by the initiative of an individual, an Islamic community, or state. The initial funding for financing the firm can be obtained from individuals, Islamic communities, state funds, or non-profit banking institutions at zero interest rate. Individuals who provide capital have the right of ownership (in the traditional sense) of the assets of the firm, but the power to control and to exploit the firm is directly related to involvement and participation of the members of the firm. Note that two questions arise during the course of this explanation. First, what is the difference between our firm and of those self-managed firms and cooperatives in socialist or capitalist economies? The answer is that unlike Islamic firms, self-managed firms and cooperatives in socialist or capitalist economies remain financially dependent on the state bureaucracies or owners of the capital. This financial reliance results in undue influence on the decision-making process of the enterprise. Thus, it is highly unrealistic to assume that members of the self-managed firms or cooperatives under contemporary economic systems can decide freely without outside influence.[3] The second question is that if the control of the Islamic firm is related to involvement and participation and not to ownership, then why would anyone be interested in supplying capital? The answer to this question is fairly

[2]The dual ownership framework is the implication of Tawhīd; the recognition that there is no God but God (Lā ilāha illā Allāh). The consciousness that Tawhīd presupposes gives men the sense of being equal while accepting God as a sole creator and ultimate owner of the universe.

[3]J. Vanek, *The General Theory of Labor-Managed Market Economies,* Chap. 15.

obvious if one understands Islamic institutions. The availability of capital at zero interest rate in the Islamic economy guarantees that an individual or community would be better off by providing their monetary assets for investment in the firm, rather than keeping them in the Islamic banks and paying transaction costs on these assets.

(ii) *Participation in Management.* The second characteristic of the Islamic economy is related to, and in a sense derived from, the first. Once the dual ownership structure is fully understood and applied, it becomes obvious that the firm members decide freely and to their best advantage on actions they take without specific outside influence such as those of capital suppliers, planning authorities, etc. However, this does not preclude general constraints, such as Islamic laws and Islamic taxation.

The main reason for this participation in management by all on the basis of equality in the Islamic economy lies in the recognition of the Sovereignty of God which essentially implies the rule of Islamic law as revealed by Him in the Qur'ān.[4] Given this law, all individuals who submit to it must be partners in its implementation. Hence, once the Sovereignty of God is recognized, the authority for its establishment is vested in the whole Ummah (Islamic Community) and is to be exercised in light of the Qur'ān through the democractic process of consultation with the Ummah as the Qur'ān states:

And consult them in affairs (3:159)
And they conduct their affairs by
mutual consultation (42:38)

(iii) *Economic Justice.* The final characteristic of the Islamic economy is economic justice. As we have already discussed in the previous chapter, the Islamic notion of dual ownership guarantees equal division of initial wealth among all members of the society. However, distribution of additional income generated by individuals or communities through work should be just, but it need not be strictly egalitarian. On the

[4](a) Is it not His to create and govern? (7:54).

(b) Sovereignty is for none but God (12:40).

(c) Follow the revelation sent to you from your Lord, and follow not, as friends or protectors, other than Him (7:3).

basis of skill and responsibilities of work, the share of the residual could be different.

2.2. Equilibrium of an Islamic Firm

The great attraction of the characteristics just mentioned above is that they permit us to derive assumptions on which a model of an Islamic economy can be based. In some respects, and especially when we formally analyze the equilibrium of the "representative" firm in an Islamic economy, these assumptions may seem somewhat similar to those discussed by Ward (1958), Domar (1966), and Vanek (1970). This is precisely because our firm, like a labor-managed firm, maximizes its net revenue per worker. But, as we shall see later, in the last analysis, it is the property rights structure in an Islamic framework, and not in any way only a firm's maximization of net revenue per worker, which makes our analysis logical, realistic, and more appealing.

2.2a. Assumptions

(i) *The Rate of Interest.* The monetary authority in the Islamic economy is assumed to maintain a zero interest rate. It is also assumed that all firms have access to a financial capital market[5] in which they can borrow at zero interest rate.

(ii) *The Firm in Relation to the Economy.* There are a large number of small firms in the Islamic economy. The link between the behavior of firms and the state of the economy is such that all firms are alike. Therefore, it is convenient to adopt the fiction of the "representative" firm.

(iii) *Free Entry.* In the Islamic economy, no artificial obstacles prevent new firms from entering, or existing firms from leaving, the industry.

(iv) *The Production Function.* A perfectly homogeneous labor is the only variable factor used by the "representative" Islamic firm, the only other being capital, fixed in supply in the short run. Thus, we have production function

$$Q = f(L|\overline{K}) \tag{1}$$

[5]By capital we mean both physical assets and their financial counterparts.

Where Q is physical output, L is variable input, and $\overline{K}$ is fixed input. The vertical bar means "given." The function $f(L|\overline{K})$ is assumed to be subject to $f'(L|\overline{K}) \geqslant 0$ and $f''(L|\overline{K}) < 0$.

(v) *Price Taking Behavior.* The "representative" Islamic firm is a price taker. The two relevant prices, that of capital, p_K and that of product, p_Q, can both be taken as given.

(vi) *Net Revenue Maximization.* In a given state faced by given p_K, and p_Q, the firm acts as to maximize net revenue (i.e., value added) per laborer on a given capital.

$$\max I = \frac{p_Q\, f(L|\overline{K}) - p_K\overline{K}}{L} \tag{2}$$

It is, however, interesting to discuss the objective function of capitalist and labor-managed firms here. The most simple description of the capitalist firm is translated by the hypothesis of profit maximization:

$$\max \pi = p_Q\, f(L|\overline{K}) - wL - r\overline{K} \tag{3}$$

Where π = profit, w = wage rate, r = rental rate of capital, i.e., price of capital, p_K, plus interest on that capital, and all other notations are the same as mentioned above.

Whereas, Ward (1958), Domar (1966), and Vanek (1970) assume that the labor-managed firm maximizes net revenue Y per worker:

$$\max Y = \frac{p_Q\, f(L|\overline{K}) - r\overline{K}}{L} \tag{4}$$

Note that rental rate of capital, r, in the labor-managed firm is identical to the rental rate of capital in the capitalist firm. Equations (2) and (4) are identical except that $p_K < r$. This is precisely the one main institutional reason that makes the Islamic firm so different from the labor-managed firm. The net revenue maximization problem of both the Islamic firm and the labor-managed firm in different socio-economic environments leads to differences in allocation of resources. We shall see this later in the chapter.

2.2b. **Equilibrium**

Maximization of equation (2) with respect to L yields:

$$I = \frac{p_Q\, f(L|\overline{K}) - p_K\overline{K}}{L} = \frac{p_Q\, \partial f(L|\overline{K})}{\partial L} \qquad (5)$$

This implies that in equilibrium the income per laborer of the Islamic firm must equal to the marginal value product of labor. This condition can also be exhibited graphically. Suppose that the production possibilities set is given in Figure 2.1. In this two-dimensional case, the total value product of labor $p_Q\, f(L|\overline{K})$, diminished by the fixed cost of capital $p_K K$, measures the total net income of labor corresponding to the various levels of employment. The net income per laborer is measured by the slope of the isoincome line.

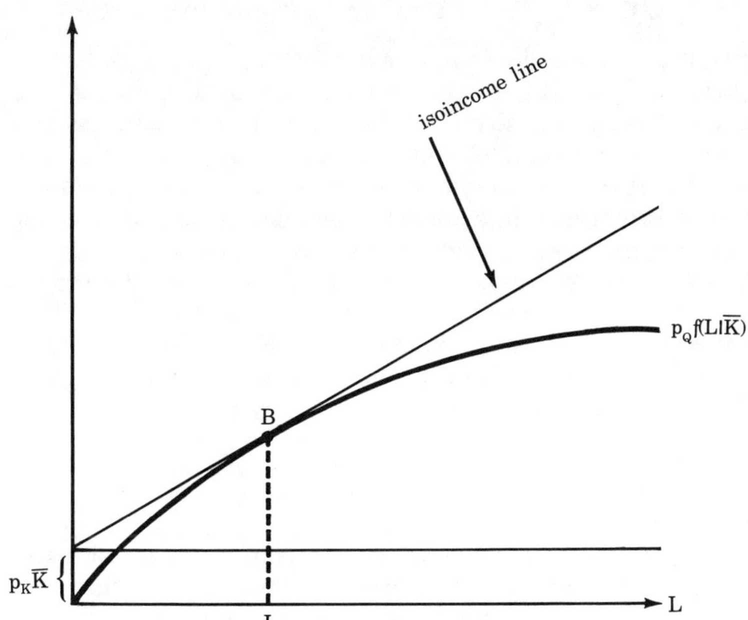

Figure 2.1

An Islamic firm wants to find out a point on the production set with the maximal level of income per laborer—this is point B where the isoincome line and contour are tangential. The case of equality among the capitalist firm, the labor-managed firm, and the Islamic firm can be obtained if, and only if,

$$r = p_K \tag{6}$$

and

$$\pi = 0 \tag{7}$$

In other words, the capitalist and the labor-managed firms are operating in a zero interest rate economy, and the capitalist firm is making zero profit. Indeed, in this case we have

$p_Q\ f(L|\overline{K}) - r\overline{K} = wL$ for the capitalist firm

$p_Q\ f(L|\overline{K}) - r\overline{K} = YL$ for the labor-managed firm

$p_Q\ f(L|\overline{K}) - p_K\overline{K} = IL$ for the Islamic firm.

Thus, marginal and average revenues are equalized, and allocation of labor is the same in each type of firm. It must be realized that at a positive interest rate in the capitalist and the labor-managed firms, both the real wage rate (in the capitalist firm) and the real net revenue per worker (in the labor-managed firm) are inferior when compared to the real net revenue per worker in the Islamic firm. The three types of laborer's income are only equal when conditions (6) and (7) are met.

In the long run, the stock of capital is variable. However, it does not make much difference in the behavior of the Islamic firm. The condition for optimality is

$$\frac{dI}{dK} = p_K \tag{8}$$

The Islamic firm always operates at that point in both the short and the long run since the short run optimization rule implies equating marginal with average revenue per unit of labor. This is also true for the labor-managed firm.

Finally, before concluding this section, we ought to address the issues related to monopolies. In the Islamic economy, all firms are bound to operate where their technologies are linear-homogeneous. Moreover, efficient firms have no incentives to grow indefinitely which essentially means less monopolistic tendencies. The reason for this is fairly obvious. The Islamic firm maximizes the average net revenue and not the total net revenue. Therefore, the point of maximum efficiency will be reached at a lower level of employment and output than in the capitalist firm and the labor-managed firm operating under capitalist or socialist economic systems. This is illustrated in Figure 2.2 and 2.3. Figure 2.2 shows optimal employment (output) level L_C of the profit maximizing capita-

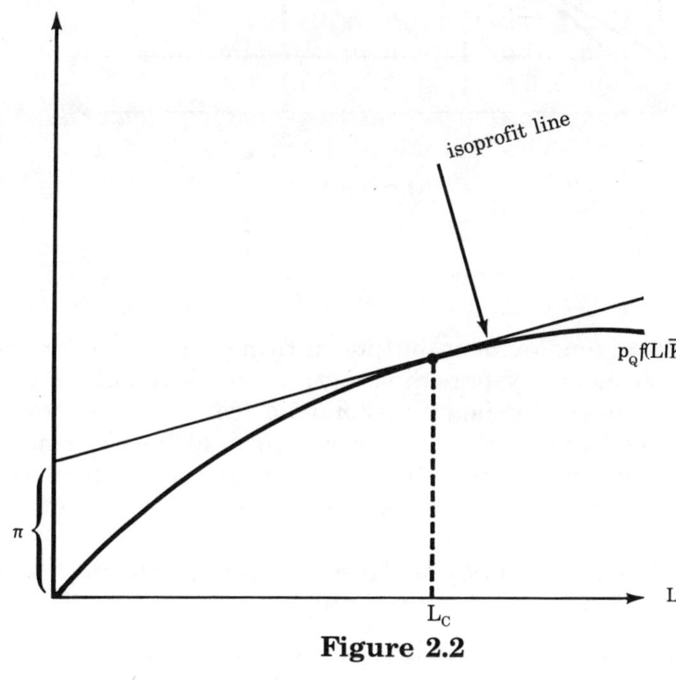

Figure 2.2

lists firm. In Figure 2.3 L_Y is the employment (output) level of labor-managered firm. Also, in the same figure, L_I shows

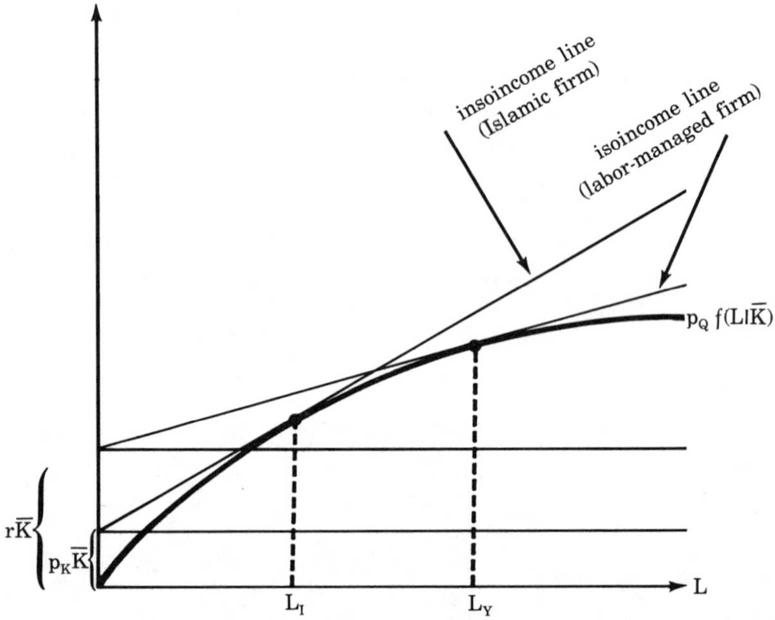

Figure 2.3

the level of employment (output) if firm operates under the Islamic economic system. Since optimal employment (output) level L_I under the Islamic economic framework is lower than the other two sytems, there is room for more firms in a given industry. Therefore, entry is far easier under the Islamic economic framework than in any other system.

2.3. Equity-Efficiency in the Islamic Economy: The General Equilibrium Analysis

So far we have discussed how the Islamic firm in equilibrium (i.e., when maximizing income for each laborer) equalizes the income of each worker category to the corresponding marginal value product. Such behavior of an Islamic firm guarantees both the optimal allocation of labor and the reasonable distribution of income of firm members, a behavior consistent with our notion of economic justice as described earlier. In this section, we shall go a step forward and discuss the issues of allocation and distribution within a general equilibrium framework. Following our usual method of comparing the different socio-economic systems, we shall see how the property rights structure within the dual ownership framework helps us in solving the issues of optimal allocation and distribution simultaneously.

2.3a. Equity and Efficiency Trade-Off: The Capitalist Economy

Consider an economy consisting of two individual farmers named Mr. A and Mr. B. Each farmer produces and consumes rice and wheat. Both farmers have identical tastes and abilities. The initial endowment of land between Mr. A and Mr.

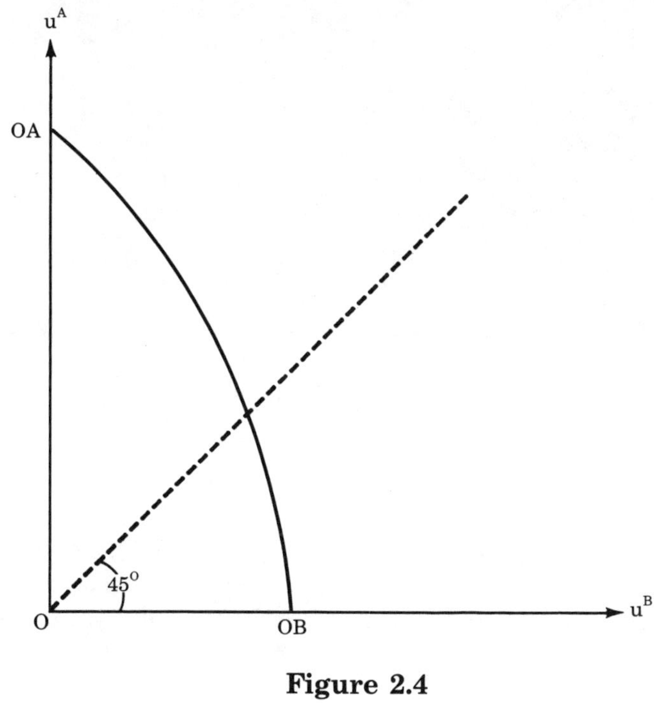

Figure 2.4

B is such that Mr. A owns more land than Mr. B. The small town economy does recognize the right of private ownership of the means of production. Allocation of resources takes place through the market and occasionally through the intervention of a government planner. Keeping in mind the initial endowment assumption, we can see that the possible distribution of land between Mr. A and Mr. B generates the curve

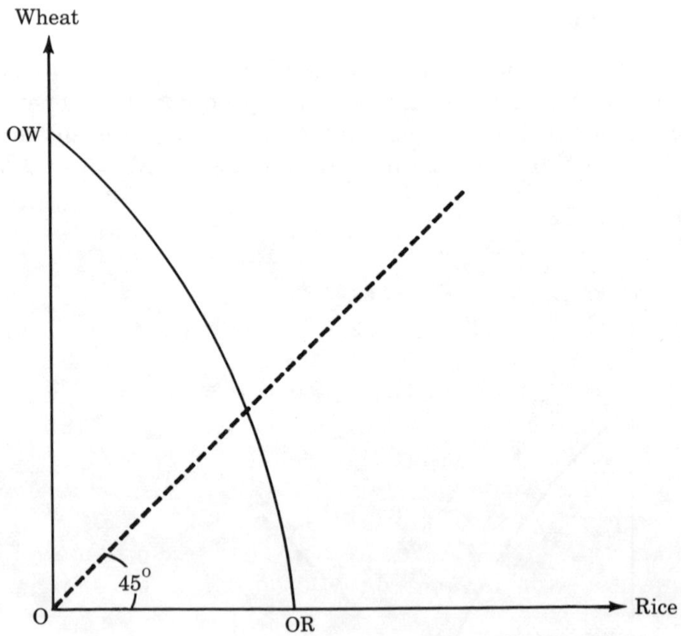

Figure 2.5

(OA,OB) in Figure 2.4, the utility possibility frontier of the small economy. Similarly, the possible output of rice and wheat by Mr. A and Mr. B generates the formally analogous curve (OR,OW) in Figure 2.5, the production possibility frontier of the simple town.

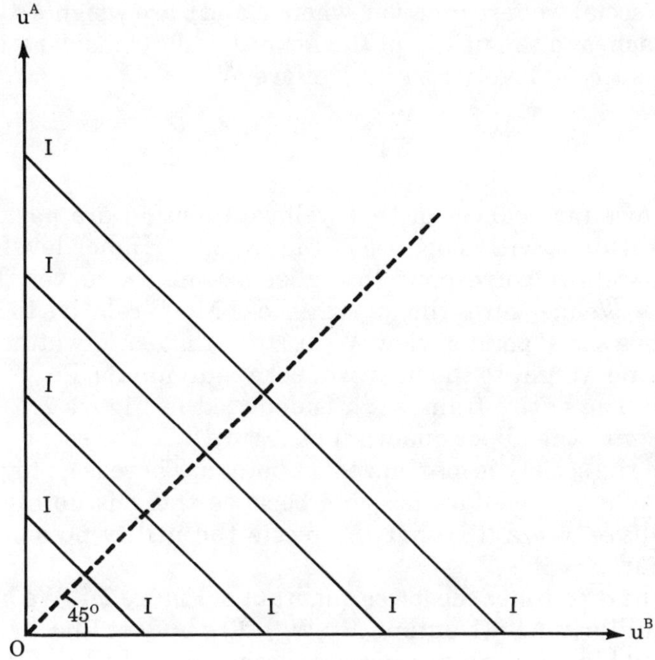

Figure 2.6

To use resources in a way deemed to be best for society requires a social welfare function.[6] Let

$$W = \alpha u^A + \beta u^B \qquad (9)$$

[6]This type of social welfare function is ethically unfounded and assumed to follow the "maximum sum of utilities" criterion, i.e., individuals are indifferent to distribution. A policy is good if the simple sum of happiness is increased. A planner is not concerned whether the gainer is already happier than the loser, provided that his gain is bigger than the loser's loss. The opposite of this criterion is "equality" criterion. Under the "equality" criterion, the planner aims at a uniform distribution of welfare and the isowelfare curves of the function would be L-shape. Between the two extremes there is a "symmetric" criterion. This implies that social valuation of an individual's welfare depends

be the social welfare function, where α and β are weights society attaches to the utility of the farmer under consideration. For a specific level of social welfare $\overline{W}$,

$$u^{A} = \frac{\overline{W}}{\alpha} - (\beta/\alpha)u^{B} \qquad (10)$$

All isowelfare curves of this welfare function are parallel straight lines with slope $-\beta/\alpha$ (Figure 2.6). Higher levels of social welfare correspond to higher isowelfare curves. The slope $-\beta/\alpha$ measures the importance of Mr. B relative to Mr. A from a social point of view. We assume that society attaches the same weight to the utility of both individuals, i.e., $-\beta/\alpha = -1$. The entire framework is depicted in Figure 2.7. We begin with the upper quadrant of Figure 2.7. The social welfare of the society is maximized[7] at point a. There is no higher state of social welfare possible because there is no higher isowelfare curve (I,I) that intersects the utility possibility frontier.

We next consider the lower quadrant of Figure 2.7. We have an equilibrium with output (R*,W*). The budget line for Mr. A's and Mr. B's conbined incomes is shown by the line (M,M). If, for example, we want to know the separate budget lines of Mr. A and Mr. B, then we measure Mr. A's budget line from O and Mr. B's budget line inward from (R*,W*). The budget line for Mr. A (referred toO) is K,K and for Mr. B (referred to L) is L,L. Since we are in equilibrium, which implies that the amount of rice demanded by Mr. A (shown at C^A) plus the amount demanded by Mr. B (shown at C^B) must add up to the total output of Rice (R*). Thus, C^A and C^B occur at the same point and total outputs (R*,W*) are demanded.

---

on the position of the individual relative to others. A "symmetric" welfare function is strictly quasi-concave in the individual utilities. Quasi-concavity guarantees isowelfare curves convex to the origin, and symmetry guarantees that they cross the 45^{0} line from the origin. Our argument in this essay will be essentially true under any of the above type welfare functions.

[7]Maximizing the social welfare function implies that nobody can increase his welfare without decreasing the welfare of somebody else, for, otherwise social welfare would not be maximum, a contradiction.

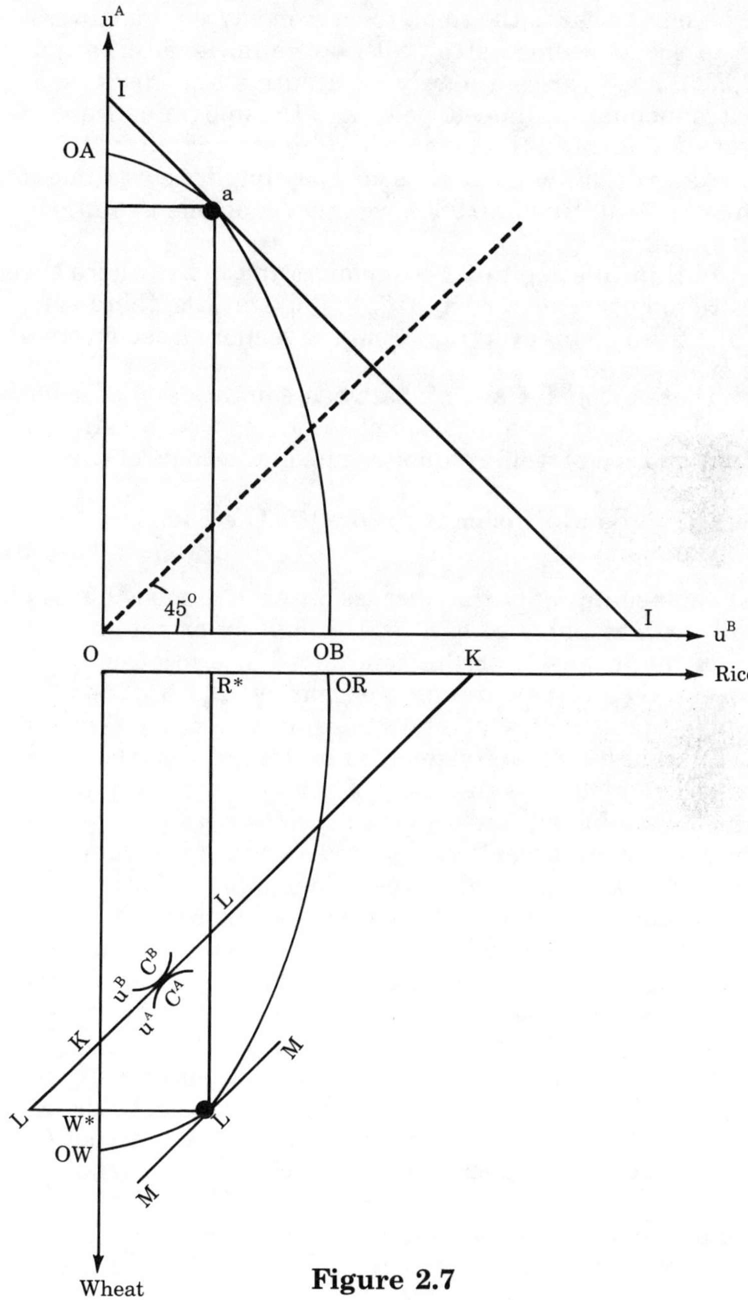

Figure 2.7

It becomes clear in the small town economy that maximization of social welfare at a, with optimum level of output (R^*,W^*), itself raises a purely distributive issue because it creates inequality. Indeed, point a in the upper quadrant of Figure 2.7 favors Mr. A and discriminates against Mr. B. Since discrimination against somebody implies curtailment of his freedom (Hayek, 1960), we must conclude two important results:

1. Within this capitalist economic framework, where the traditional private property right view prevails, there is no perfect freedom for everyone. Some have more freedom than the others; and
2. There exists a trade-off between equality and efficiency in the sense that allocation of resources that maximizes output and social welfare implies unequal income of equals.

2.3b. **Equity and Efficiency Trade-Off: The Socialist Economy**

At the beginning of this discussion we assumed that the small town economy recognizes the right of private ownership of the means of production, and that allocation of resources takes place through the market and occasionally through the intervention of a government planner. We can relax that assumption. Instead, let us assume that the small town economy denies the right of private ownership of the means of production and reserves such ownership to public bodies. Furthermore, allocation of resources and income distribution depend primarily on central planning. The socialist planner controls almost all phases of economic life.

The objective of the socialist planner is to use resources in a way which enhances equitable distribution of income and efficiency. One of the best considered alternatives to achieve equality is redistribution. The asymmetry in the utility possibility frontier and production possibility frontier arises because of the difference in the initial endowments. In section 2.3a, the initial endowments were so skewed that even perfect efficient trading (Figure 2.7) insured a relatively unequal outcome of utilities.

Let us suppose that the socialist planner can change initial endowments through redistribution. This will change the utility possibility frontier and production possibility frontier from asymmetric to symmetric. But, the centralization combined with this redistribution policy by the socialist planner will give rise to a series of problems concerning inefficiencies, low productivity, and a lack of work incentives, which cause shrinkage of both possibility frontiers. The reasons are two-fold: first, if the socialist planner keeps the products prices constant, an increase in the initial endowment of Mr. B through a centralization-cum-redistribution policy will lead to an increase in Mr. B's level of satisfaction with increasing output at a decreasing rate. The increasing output at a decreasing rate is clearly caused by a lack of work incentive. This happens because Mr. B will not increase his output beyond a certain limit, partly due to the income effect of Mr. A that leads to a reduced demand for the total output in the economy, and partly due to the price ceiling imposed by the socialist planner on Mr. B's output. Second, at constant prices, a decrease in the initial endowment of Mr. A will lead to a decrease in his level of satisfaction with decreasing output at an increasing rate. The rationale behind decreasing output at an increasing rate is very simple. The redistribution that attaches more weight to the utility of Mr. B than to that of Mr. A generates discrimination. This discrimination leads to a lack of motivation and work incentives, a situation which adversely affects Mr. A's efficiency and productivity. This implies that the output of Mr. A decreases due to his reduced initial endowment at the first round, and the output decreases at an increasing rate due to the increasing lack of incentives and motivations caused by discrimination at the second round.

To elaborate the above ideas, consider Figure 2.8. The new symmetric utility possibility frontier (OA′, OB ′) and the new symmetric production possibility frontier (OR′, OW′) are shown in the upper and lower quadrant, respectively. The new budget line for Mr. A's and Mr. B's combined incomes (M′, M′) in the lower quadrant is lower than the original budget line (M, M). The budget line (M′, M′) in the lower quadrant will correspond to the isowelfare curve (I′,I′) in the upper quadrant. The isowelfare curve (I′,I′) is inferior to curve (I,I) in the sense that a lower isowelfare curve corresponds to a lower social welfare. Note that at the new equilibrium point E, equality is achieved because the lower isowelfare

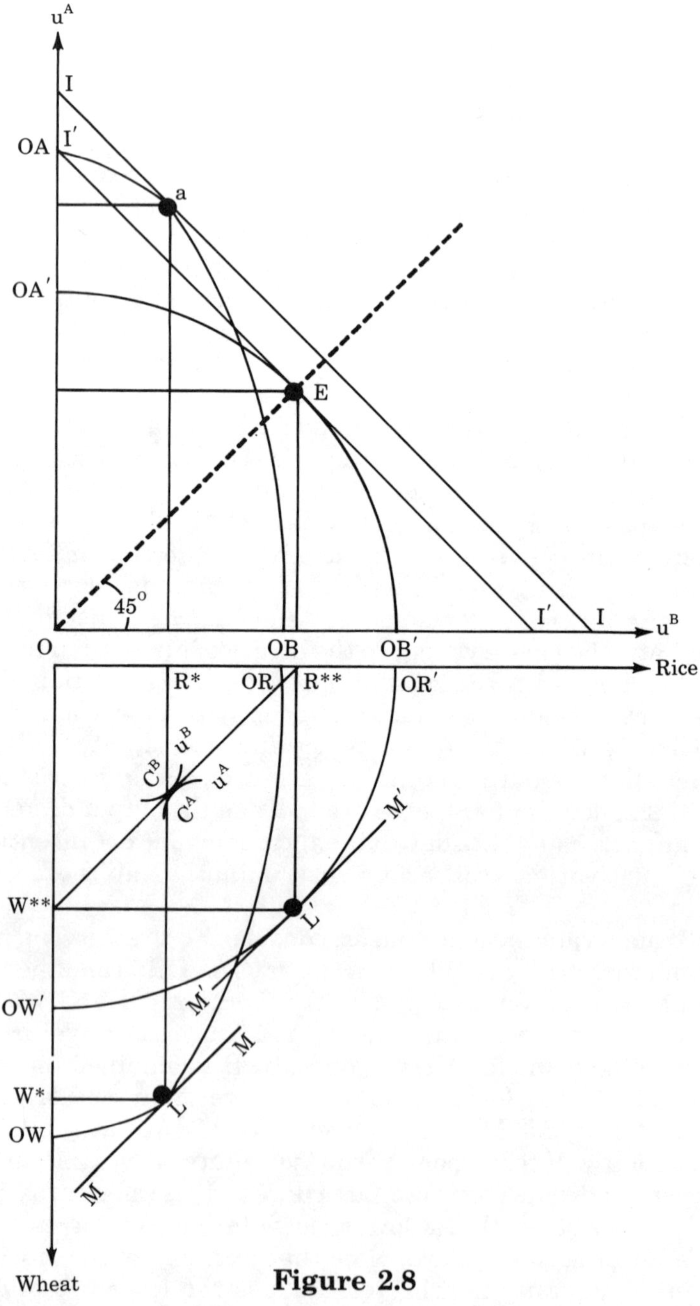

u^A
I
OA
I′
a
OA′
E
45°
O
OB
OB′
I′
I
u^B
Rice
R*
OR
R**
OR′
C^B
u^B
u^A
C^A
M′
W**
L′
OW′
M′
M
W*
L
OW
M
Wheat

Figure 2.8

curve (I′, I′) becomes tangent to the utility possibility frontier (OA′, OB′) at its intersection with the 45°—angle line. However, it must be recognized that such equity in income is achieved not only at the cost of efficiency but also at the cost of discrimination against Mr. A. Thus, there exists no mechanism in a socialist framework that guarantees simultaneous efficiency and equitable distribution of income.

2.3c. **Equity and Efficiency in the Islamic Economy**

So far we have noted that the government planner under the capitalist economic system and the socialist planner under socialist economic structures sought to use resources in a way deemed best for the society. Yet each planner failed to provide simultaneously equitable distribution of income and efficiency for their societies. The purpose of this section is to attempt to explore the possibilities of achieving equity and efficiency simultaneously under the Islamic economic system in a small town economy.

Suppose now that all other assumptions are left intact except that our small town economy rejects both contemporary economic systems in favor of an Islamic economic system. The small town economy under an Islamic economic system can rightly be called an Islamic economy if: (a) the economy follows the dual ownership framework and thus allows the legal right of private ownership of the means of production, but, this right can be legitimately earned only through labor; (b) the community as a whole discuss, debate, and determine the distribution and allocation of resources; (c) the economy is fully decentralized in the sense that all decision-making units, firms, households, associations, communities, and public sectors decide freely without direct outside interference; and (d) the human factor is not merely a factor of production, but also of decision-making, an innovative and enterpreneural factor.

Under an Islamic economic system, the redistribution-cum-decentralization policy of the Muslim planner[8] will result in a symmetric production possibility frontier and utility pos-

[8]The Muslim planner simply represents the preferences of the community and the possibilities of his action depend upon the will of the

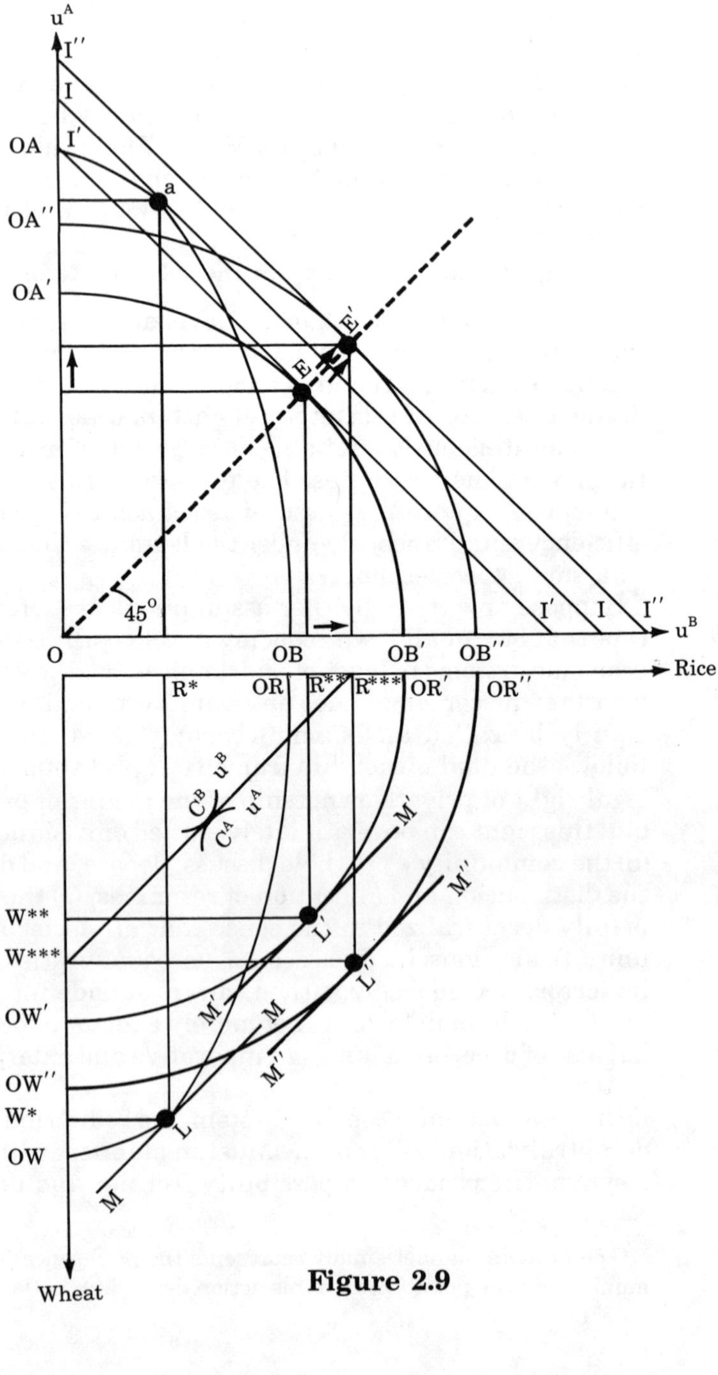

u^A
I''
I
I'
OA
a
OA''
OA'
E'
E
45°
I'
I
I''
u^B
O
OB
OB'
OB''
Rice
R*
OR
R**
R***
OR'
OR''
C^B
u^B
u^A
C^A
M'
M''
W**
L'
W***
L''
OW'
M'
M
M''
OW''
W*
L
OW
M
Wheat

Figure 2.9

sibility frontier (Figure 2.9). This new symmetric production possibility frontier (OR$''$, OW$''$) is superior to previous ones in the sense that it becomes tangent to the higher budget line (M$''$, M$''$) of the combined incomes of Mr. A and Mr. B. Similarly, the new utility possibility frontier (OA$''$, OB$''$) is also superior to the old ones as it generates a higher level of social welfare. This happens because (a) under the capitalist economic system, due to unequal initial endowments, opulent Mr. A obtains less marginal satisfaction from the use of resources than does poor Mr. B; (b) under the socialist economic system, centralization policy of the socialist planner gives rise to inefficiencies, low productivity, and a lack of incentives which are reflected in the shrinkage of the production possibility curve and the utility possibility curve; and (c) under the Islamic economic system, after redistribution combined with decentralization, the loss of satisfaction will be outweighed by the corresponding gain. At the new equilibrium point E$'$, equality and efficiency are both achieved because the higher isowelfare curve (I$''$, I$''$) becomes tangent to the utility possibility frontier (OA$''$, OB$''$) at its intersection with the 45°-angle line. Thus, the distribution and the allocation of resources in the Islamic economy is a neat, manageable problem to which economic techniques can be applied with maximum advantage. Note that our result is far more general than this discussion tends to suggest.

2.4. Conclusions and Summary

In this chapter our emphasis has been primarily on the issues of allocation and distribution. We have presented an economic model of the Islamic firm and shown that the Islamic firm in equilibrium equalizes the income of each worker category to the corresponding marginal value product. We argued that optimal resource allocation in the Islamic economy involves both technical economic efficiency and ethical value consideration as essential elements for economic justice. The analytical framework presented in sections 2.3a and 2.3b demonstrates that capitalist and socialist economic systems

society he represents. By contrast, the socialist planner is omnipotent and the possibilities of action entirely open to him.

fail to achieve equity and efficiency simultaneously. By contrast, the Islamic economic system (section 2.3c) appears to be far superior to any other system in existence. In the sphere of allocative efficiency, it is at worst equal to the capitalist economic system, while it is definitely better than socialism. As far as the efficient but "just" pattern of income and wealth distribution is concerned, it is definitely superior to both systems.

3

The Libyan Experience Viewed Through the Theory of Islamic Economics

Throughout modern economic history, economists and social scientists have been confronted with the problem of liberating the working man from the capitalist. The pursuit of this goal has proven to be a difficult undertaking. Of the many ideas advanced by the social scientists, socialism was the only system that succeeded in gaining a significant world acceptance as an alternative to capitalism. Although socialism liberated the working man from the individual capitalist, it failed to liberate him from the collective capitalist. Thus, the central problem of liberation remained unsolved despite years of intellectual inquiry.

While efforts to find a viable solution were focused elsewhere, the Islamic economic system awaited recognition of its potential to deliver the heretofore unfulfilled objectives. It had long advocated and provided for the emancipation of working men from both forms of servitude: the collective as well as the individual capitalist.

In recent years, the Islamic economic system has gained visible acceptance in Libya. It is by no means a full scale implementation of the Islamic economic system. But its significance lies in the fact that it has found an avenue where it can be translated into an even more developed framework.

3.1. The Nature of the Libyan Experience

The constitutional declaration instituting the people's authority and the workers' participation in the decision-making process was issued in Libya on 2 Shawal, 1389 H., corresponding to December 11, 1969, and the economy made a rapid transition to that system. By April, 1973, the workers' participation, both in management through their new status from workers to partners and in the income of enterprises, was the main operating principal in the production process.

To explain the system more specifically, let us consider that a firm in Libya can be created by the initiative of either the Public Administration or a local community. Once created—building built and machines installed—the firm assumes a life of its own in the sense that the power to control and exploit the firm rests in the association of the working community and not in any way in those who may have provided the capital assets. Also, such a firm remains fully autonomous as long as it fulfills the general legal and financial obligations applicable to all firms in the economy. The principal elected decision-making body is the workers' council, named the People's Committee. The committee consists of a group of workers called upon by all workers to carry out day-to-day tasks. Thus, the committee is an instrument guaranteeing the implementation of decisions taken from the working community concerning the policy of the enterprise. Among these decisions are the determination of the income distribution schedule and other basic statutes of the firm, the major acquisitions or sales of the physical plant and equipment, and the appointment or vote of confidence in the secretary. The secretary of the enterprise is normally elected by the People's Committee and approved by the working community of the enterprise. In his actions, however, the secretary is entirely responsible to the working collective of his firm. In his external acts, he is bound to uphold the general rules and laws regulating the enterprise, such as those regarding taxation, financial reporting, and fulfillment of debt-service obligations.

We may now briefly go over the basic defining characteristics of the Libyan system in light of the characteristics of the Islamic economic system.

(i) *Dual Ownership.* An Islamic economy is unlikely to be one in which all economic activity is either privately owned or nationalized. It will be a "unique economy," combining private ownership, state ownership, and social ownership, and incorporating different degrees of state, consumers', and workers' control within the dual ownership framework. In this spectrum, the Libyan practice is different from our theoretical model. In the Libyan firm, the working community has the exclusive right to control and to manage its activities and has absolutely no right of ownership of the capital assets which it uses. The working community can enjoy the fruits of production for which the plant and equipment are used, but it must pay for this a contractual fee or rent to the state. In turn, the state has no right of control whatsoever over the physical assets of the firm as long as the working community meets all its legal, institutional, and financial obligations. Therefore, the Libyan firm does not generate its capital nor can the firm members sell the real assets and distribute the proceeds as current income.

This reliance on financing from only one external source, namely, the "state," differs from what we have given as our first defining characteristic of the Islamic economy. According to our definition, capital assets of the firm can be financed either from retained earnings or from borrowed funds, ultimately to be repaid from retained earnings. This is a crucial point since it can easily be demonstrated that the financing of capital by the state, without an adequate opportunity cost, can lead to misallocation of resources, an event which frequently happens in Libya.

(ii) *Participation in Management.* Participation in management is a major concern of the industrial democracies since the last decade, and it has been much discussed among economists in the West. However, there is no general agreement on the definition of the concept itself. There are those who view it as the alteration of the capitalist system of ownership. Others maintain it to be synonymous with "industrial democracy," interpreting the latter concept in different ways. Still others, departing from practice, hold it to be identical to selected modes of actual participation procedures, such as profit sharing or work councils.

The Islamic economic system presented in previous chapters clearly defines the concept: participation in management by all on the basis of equality through democratic process, which essentially implies equal partnership in the firm. In this light, the Libyan economy is unquestionably similar to the Islamic economy. The workers' participation in management, through their changing status from workers to partners, is taken as a measure of multiple application of democracy and an indication of societal decentralization.

(iii) *Economic Justice.* In the last characteristic economic justice, there is no major difference between the Libyan model and our theoretical one. The income generated by the firm is distributed according to each workers' contribution.

3.2. Planning Activities within the Libyan Experience

Planning for economic and social development constitutes the best means for the allocation and proper utilization of resources so as to achieve optimum welfare for the society in the shortest possible time. However, the success of development planning as a means to achieve optimum welfare objectives in a particular country always depends on its compatibility with the nature of the socio-economic system of that country.

In compliance with this principle, the Libyan development plans are designed by all social and economic forces who later put the plan into practice, and thereby the application of the principle of "Partners, Not Wage Workers" is fully realized.

The relationship of the Secretariat of Planning to the Central Bank, popular Congresses, People's Committees, unions, syndicates, and to professional associations, as it goes about its preparatory and advisory duties pursuant to the central economic plan, is intricate. As Figure 3.1 indicates, the Secretariat of Planning both gives and receives information and

The Relationship of the Secretariat of Planning to Other Institutions

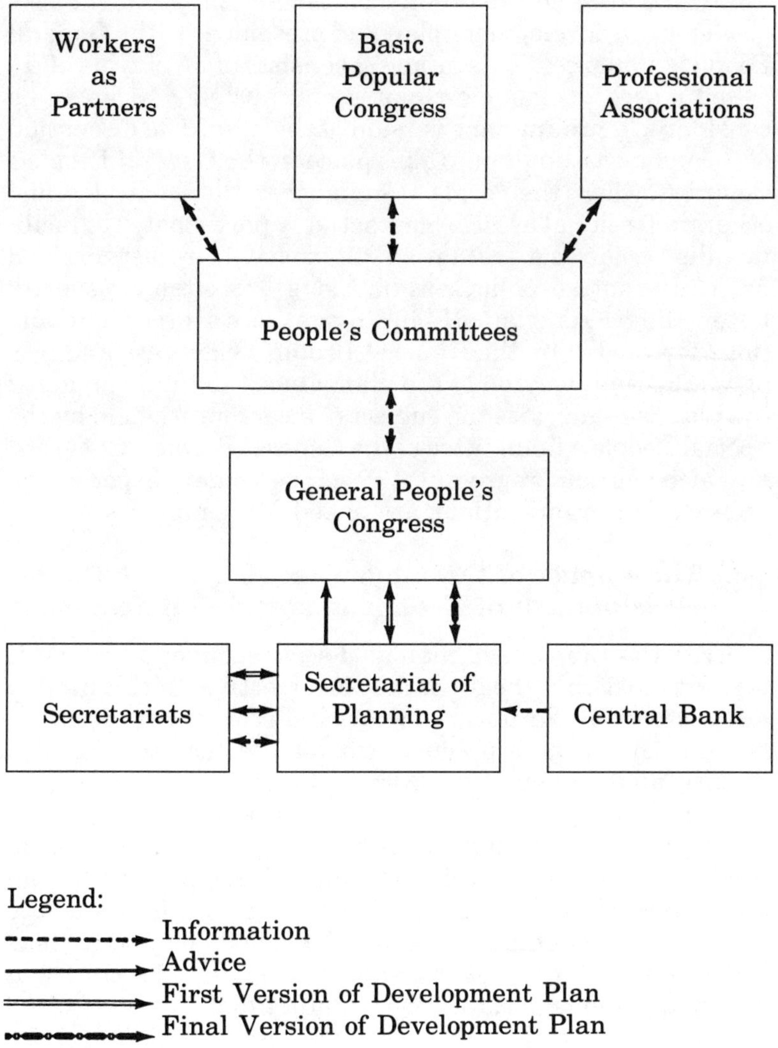

Figure 3.1

advice relevant to the plan. Certain aspects of these relationships and activities leading up to the final version of the plan have become institutionalized.

The Secretariat of Planning, with the collaboration of the Central Bank and the other secretariats, prepares the proposal for the development plan and presents it to the General People's Congress. This proposal consists of an outline of so-called macro-economic estimates and targets which can be considered a preliminary version of the plan. The discussion of the policy assumptions takes place in the General People's Congress, where the People's Committees, the syndicates, and other professional associations actively participate. To facilitate discussion and evaluation, alternative forecasts derived from alternative policy assumptions are often presented. Later, the Secretariat of Planning gathers all recommendations forwarded by the General People's Congress and prepares the final version of the plan. Once the final version of the plan is ready, it is the subject of a conference held by the Special People's Committee of the General People's Congress, at which workers' representatives, independent experts, and professional organizations are asked for comments.

3.3. The Impact of the Libyan Experience on the Development of Economic and Social Sectors

Given the Libyan self-managed socio-economic system, it is fairly clear that the fundamental objectives of this system are to steadily transform the national economy from the oil sector to the dynamic productive non-oil sectors, such as agriculture and industry, in order to build Libya into a self-sufficient state, along with the promotion of higher growth rates and the equitable distribution of income and wealth. But, is such a system at all the vehicle of economic and social development? And, if so, to what extent does it contribute positively? A closer look at the development of productive non-oil economic sectors and, of course, various social sectors will clarify questions both of theory and of fact.[1]

[1]Most of the data that we will use regarding the development of these sectors has been assembled by the Secretariat of Planning and compiled in the *Economic and Social Transformation Plan* (1976-1980) and (1981-1985).

3.3a. **Agriculture**

The Libyan Arab Jamahiriya, after the outbreak of the September Revolution, attached a high priority to agricultural development in order to achieve self-sufficiency. The Council of Land Reclamation and Development was formed on October 10, 1972, in order to achieve the following aims:

1. Preservation and proper exploitation of natural resources, water, soil, and forests.
2. Participation in the progress of the national economy by means of increasing agricultural products which aims at realizing self-sufficiency in cereals and meat.
3. Efforts to create residential communities in agricultural areas by providing the means which guarantee an adequate standard of living.

During the First Development Plan (1973-1975), agriculture received a higher priority than any other sector. Although the original amount allocated was L.D. 566.1 million, the total amount invested in agricultural development projects only reached about L.D. 526.7 million by the end of December, 1975. Within these three years, remarkable progress in agricultural production occurred. For instance, the quantity of meat produced until the end of the plan period amounted to 46,000 tons. Milk and barley amounted to 85,000 and 216,000 tons, respectively. It was also during the three year plan period that the implementation of several agricultural development projects, such as Al-Jefara, Al-Jabal Al-Akhdar, Fezzan, Al-Kafra, Wal-Sareer and Al-Soloul Al-Khodra, were started. The horizontal expansion of these projects in terms of new areas contributed to a remarkable increase in the agricultural production of the main crops. Table 3.1 shows the agricultural production of the main crops in 1975 as distributed over the cultivated areas before the Plan and the new areas during the Plan.

The Second Development Plan (1976-1980) initially allocated L.D. 1,226.6 million for the agricultural development sector and subsequently revised the amount to L.D. 1,888.0 million, but this increase in the development budget was not reflected in any increase in the program targets. As compared to this revised outlay, L.D. 1,637.9 million (about 87%) were actually spent (see Table 3.2). The production of agricultural

Table 3.1

Agricultural Production of Main Crops, 1975

(1000 tonnes)

Crops	Total Production	Land Cultivated Before the Plan		New Land During the Plan	
		Quantity of Production	Proportion to the Sector	Quantity or Production	Proportion to the Sector
Wheat	107	73	68%	34	32%
Barley	216	188	87%	28	13%
Legumes	8	6	75%	2	25%
Vegetables	620	485	78%	135	22%
Fruit	130	125	96%	5	4%
Meat	46	37	80%	9	20%
Milk	85	49	58%	36	42%
Eggs	9	6.5	72%	2.5	28%

Source: Secretariat of Planning, Socialist People's Libyan Arab Jamahirya, *The Economic and Social Transformation Plan* (1976-1980), Part 2, p. 6.

Table 3.2

Development Expenditure in Agriculture, 1976-1980

(Million L.D. in current prices)

Secretariat*	1976	1977	1978	1979	1980	Plan (1976-1980)		
							Budget	
	Actual					Actual	Original	Revised
Agriculture	102.5	100.3	107.8	116.9	147.9	575.4	445.3	481.9
Land Reclamation and Reconstruction	182.8	158.6	160.0	219.0	271.0	991.4	781.3	1261.5
Dams and Water Resources	3.1	4.8	12.0	20.1	31.1	71.1	—	136.6
TOTAL	288.4	263.7	279.8	356.0	450.0	1,637.9	1,226.6	1,8880.0

*All the three Secretariats were merged in 1980. The distribution is based on the sectors handled by each of them earlier.

Source: Secretariat of Planning, Socialist People's Libyan Arab Jamahiriya, *The Economic and Social Transformation Plan* (1981-1985), Vol. I, p. 41.

commodities during this period fell far short of planned targets. The implementation ratio ranged from 30.0% in legumes and nuts to 68.4% in fruits and 75.4% in olive oil (see Table 3.3).

The overall achievements of the agricultural sector during the First Development Plan (1973-1975) were encouraging and optimism prevailed that Libya would soon be self-sufficient in the agricultural sector. However, this tide of hope disappeared when the Second Development Plan (1976-1980) failed to achieve planned targets (shown in Table 3.3) and productivity declined throughout these years. The unsatisfactory results during these years may be due to a number of factors, such as ambitious production targets, unfavorable weather conditions, and inadequate infrastructure, or it may simply be due to lack of sufficient work incentives within the socio-economic framework of Libya.

3.3b. **The Manufacturing Industry**

The manufacturing industrial sector is of special importance in the development strategy of the Libyan Arab Jamahiriya. This is due to the crucial role it has to play in the process of transforming and restructuring the economy by progressively decreasing the degree of dependence on the oil sector.

Prior to the recent socio-economic system of Libya, the manufacturing industry played only a marginal role in the national economy. Studies of the main economic variables (production, income, and investment) reveal slow growth rates and their ineffective contribution to the national economy, as well as the thinner national industrial output which rendered it unable to supply the main domestic needs. During the period 1964-1970, due to a slow growth rate, the share of the manufacturing industry in GDP was only 1.09. It was only after 1970 that industrial development began to be more and more significant.

Industrialization was one of the main objectives of the First Development Plan (1973-1975). This plan was characterized by highly intensive investments. The industrial sector received large volumes of fixed investment in accordance with the objectives of the plan. The share of gross fixed capital formation in manufacturing industries was about 13% of the

Table 3.3

Production of Important Agricultural Commodities During the Development Plan, 1976-1980

(1000 tonnes)

	Based year (1975)		Target 1980	Achievement 1980	Implementation Ratio
Commodity	Original	Revised			
Wheat	107	75	336	122.4	36.3
Barley	216	192	245	82.0	33.5
Fruits	130	128	255	160.0	62.7
Vegetables	620	564	825	564.0	68.4
Legumes & Nuts	24	19	42	12.6	30.0
Olive oil	18	18	37	27.9	75.4
Fodders	616	351	1,321	450	34.1
Meat	46	38	98	53.7	54.8
Milk	85	87	290	110	37.9
Eggs	9	10.3	25	15.7	62.8
Honey	0.35	0.235	0.6	0.360	60.0
Fisheries	4.70	4.70	11.0	4.00	36.4

Source: Secretariat of Planning, Socialist People's Libyan Arab Jamahiriya, *The Economic and Social Transformation Plan* (1981-1985). Vol. 1, p. 43.

total fixed investment made during the three year plan. Thus, the implementation of this plan brought about considerable increase in the production of a large number of industrial commodities. For instance, the production of dairy products increased from 20 million litres in 1972 to 28 million litres in 1975, flour from 77,000 tons to 158,700 tons, cement from 60,000 tons to 550,000 tons and fodders from 25,000 tons to 55,000 tons, respectively. This plan also included 74 industrial projects of which 24 projects, covering different fields of production, were completed: 9 projects for the food processing industry, 5 for the textile and leather industry, 1 for the wood and furniture industry, 1 in the petroleum refining industry, 5 in the building materials industry, and 3 in the metal and electrical equipment industries. However, the share of the manufacturing industry in the total fixed capital formation did not exceed more than 14%, and the share in total employment was only about 4.8%. As a result, total manufacturing output in terms of value added reached a relatively modest figure of 65.5 million L.D. in 1975 which represents 1.8% of the total GDP generated in that year.

During the period of the Second Development Plan (1976-1980), 44 new industrial plants were constructed and put into operation (see Table 3.4). In December 1978, 42 projects were under construction, 10 under contracting, and 31 under study (see Table 3.5). Out of these, 24 projects were expected to be completed by 1980 (see Table 3.6). Despite these very intensive activities in the field of the implementation of new industrial units, the growth of manufacturing industries during the plan period 1976-1980, was expected to be slower than planned. As against the projected gross value added of L.D. 323.4 million by 1980 (an average annual growth rate of 30.7%), the actual achievement was estimated to be only L.D. 170.6 million (at constant 1975 prices) giving an annual growth rate of 21.1%. Excluding the petroleum products, the two figures work out at 25.0% and 16.1%, respectively.

The Secretariat of Planning believes that one of the major constraints affecting implementation of planned development of the manufacturing sector is the failure of the agricultural sector to supply sufficient quantities of raw materials for new food processing industries. Lack of technical power, organiza-

Table 3.4

New Industrial Plants Put into Operation

Industry Groups and Subgroups	Number of units
Food Processing:	
flour mills, animal feed, sardine canning, vegetables and fruits, dates, syrup and baby food	13
Beverages:	
Soft drinks	1
Tobacco:	
Cigarettes Factory	1
Textiles and Leather:	
dyeing, wool washing and weaving, pressed leather tanning, sport and military foot wear production	4
Paper and Printing:	
Printing house and cement paper bags	2
Petroleum products:	
Zawia refinery	1
Petrochemicals:	
Ammonia, methanol and urea	3
Building materials:	
cement, lime, glassware, tiles, ceramics, sanitary ware, bricks, eternite pipes	13
Metallurgy:	
Scrap smelting	1
Metal and electrical equipment:	
cables and wires, pipes, tin unit and liquid batteries	5
Total	44

Source: Secretariat of Planning, Socialist People's Libyan Arab Jamahiriya, *The Economic and Social Transformation Plan* (1981-1985), Vol 1. p. 55.

Table 3.5

Industrial Plants under Construction, Contracting, and Study

Industry Groups	Under Construction	Under Contracting or Study	Total
—Food industries	13	9	22
—Textiles and leather	3	4	7
—Wood and furniture	2	—	2
—Paper and printing	1	1	2
—Chemicals	6	9	15
—Petroleum products	1	—	2
—Petrochemicals	4	3	7
—Building materials	5	2	7
—Metallurgy	2	—	2
—Metal and electrical equipment	5	13	15
Total	42	41	83

Source: Secretariat of Planning, Socialist People's Libyan Arab Jamahiriya, *The Economic and Social Transformation Plan* (1981-1985), Vol. I, p. 56.

Table 3.6

Industrial Plants Expected to be Completed by 1980

Industry Groups and Subgroups	Number of projects
—Food Industries:	
Mills, date packing, fruit complex, long macaroni and animal feed	6
—Textiles and leather:	
Blanket production, cotton wool, bandages and gauzes and tanning	3
—Wood and furniture:	
Furniture	1
—Chemicals:	
Tyres, chemical complex, waste processing units, soap	6
—Petroleum products:	
Asphalt production	1
—Petrochemicals:	
Urea	1
—Building materials:	
Cement and lime	2
—Matallurgy:	
Rolling mill	1
—Metal and electrical equipment:	
Irrigation pipes, tractors assembly, central maintenance workshop	3
Total	24

Source: Secretariat of Planning, Socialist People's Libyan Arab Jamahiriya, *The Economic and Social Transformation Plan* (1981-1985), Vol. I, p. 57.

tional and managerial skills, and experience have also contributed to the lower than planned growth of the manufacturing sector during the Second Development Plan period. Insufficient work incentive and inadequate experience in marketing may also have caused low demand for industrial products, hence, slackening the pace of industrialization in the country.

3.3c **Housing**

In Libya, the provision of adequate and healthy housing is considered one of the main objectives of the new socio-economic system. To the Revolutionary Government, housing is a social necessity which involves the satisfaction of a basic need of the individual, and it ranks third after food and clothing. The government also believes that the provision of better housing conditions for the people, coupled with an equitable distribution of the available housing facilities, is one of the incentives which encourages people to work efficiently for the acceleration of the development process in all fields of economic and social activities. Furthermore, since investment in the residential buildings constitutes a large size of the output of the construction sector, the processing of housing construction would thus contribute to expanding the pool of the work force engaged in construction, which is made of a heterogenous variety of skilled and semi-skilled trades. The housing loans would naturally expand the demand for goods and services. The outcome of this process is constant economic growth leading to a rise in the standard of living of the society.

Accordingly, the self-managed socio-economic system in Libya paid much attention to legislative regulations related to housing. It devised an independent sector for housing beginning with the "Housing Secretariat" to the public establishment for housing (which was later annexed to the Housing Secretariat), the public sector of construction companies, and the housing cooperatives. In addition to this, the Revolutionary Government issued advance housing legislation that tackled the problem and devised solutions for the housing matters. Following is a review of regulations and legislative enactments:

1. A decree for reducing rents, later replaced by the 1976

Law No. 28. Its aim was to establish a just relation between the proprietor and the tenant. Its main rulings included defining the proper rent, avoiding arbitrary evictions, and providing special attention to the needs of tenants with limited incomes.

2. The issuance of a bill for regulating the rent of the state buildings, distributing them justly among those who deserve them, and reducing rents of such buildings for the benefit of families with limited incomes.

3. Implementing the main recommendations of the people's conferences, notably, exempting any person whose monthly income is less than L.D. 100 from payment of ownership installments or loans which had been obtained for the purpose of building a house.

4. After issuing several laws related to the sale of public dwellings, a bill was issued on January 17, 1979 laying down reasonable prices for state-owned dwellings. Buyers whose monthly income was less than LD. 500 were exempted from repaying any amount over L.D. 12,000 of the total cost of the house. Also, every buyer was exempted from paying a part of the installment sum if this part would reduce his income to less than LD. 100. In all cases, sales were made on the basis of long-term installments over a period of 20 years.

The legislative enactments coupled with significant activity in housing construction during the period of the First and Second Development Plans were considered a major achievement of the system, an achievement which might lead to economic and social justice for the whole society. Total contracts concluded by the various governmental authorities for the construction of 80 thousand houses during the First Development Plan (1973-1975) amounted in value to about L.D. 722 million. Loans extended to individuals in the private sector for the same purpose amounted to about L.D. 300 million and were meant to build nearly 50 thousand houses. The number of new dwelling units implemented during the 1973-1975 Plan was about 76 thousand, against the projected 90 thousand representing an implementation percentage of 84%. The share of the public sector in the implemented housing construction was 36 thousand units, or 50% of the approved total of 64 thousand units. But of these, about 34 thousand units or 94% of the share of the public sector, were constructed by the public housing corporation. The private sector constructed much more (40 thousand houses) than initially approved (26 thousand) for it during the First Development Plan. As a consequence of the completion of these houses during the three year plan, the congestion ratio of the existing houses was reduced from 1.14 households per house in 1973 to 1.017 households per house in 1975. Also, the ratio of house constructed during the years 1973-1975 reached 11 per thousand people.

The tempo of housing construction during the Second Development Plan (1976-1980) slowed down substantially, and the average annual rate of construction of housing units was only 15,563 with 59,952 units under construction by the end of 1980. Under the Second Development Plan, out of the target of 145,000 housing units, the public sector was originally given the task of constructing 80,550 units (53.7%), and the private sector was expected to complete 64,450 units (46.3%). This is in addition to the completion of the backlogged 25,531 housing units then under construction by the end of the First Development Plan, 1973-1975.

Table 3.7 shows the role played by each implementing and coordinating agency in housing construction during the Second Development Plan period. It can be seen that during the period 1976-1980, only 31,072 housing units were completed directly by public agencies, which represented 44% of the revised planned target of 70,000 units for the public sector. By completing 46,747 units, the private sector accomplished 58% of its revised target of 80,000 units. Thus, during the Second Development Plan, with a total of 77,819 units completed by both public and private sectors, the overall average annual rate of completion was 15,563 units, and overall rate of implementation of the program stood at 52%.

In 1975, with only 330,000 standard dwelling units for 428,000 settled familes, the shortage remained at 98,000 units. The failure to implement the planned target during 1976-1980 worsened the housing situation as is seen in Table 3.8.

The adverse housing situation might be blamed on higher population growth rates which remained at 4% during 1975-1980. But the fact is that the participation of the private sector diminished constantly during this period and efficiency

Table 3.7

Activity in Housing Construction by the Public and Private Sectors

Public Sector	No. of Units completed during 1976-1980	No. of Units under const. by end of 1980
1. Secretariat of Housing	28,381	32,237
2. Secretariat of Reclamation and Reconstruction	2,307	26
3. Secretariat of Health	—	640
4. Secretariat of Education	—	500
5. Secretariat of Electricity & Water	—	280
6. Secretariat of Social Security	384	4,032
7. Additional Units to be constructed as per decision of the General People's Committee	—	11,000
Sub-total, Public Sector	31,072	48,715
Construction Through Private Initiative		
1. Housing Societies	11,534	9,737
2. Real Estate Banks	17,946	1,500
3. Commercial Banks	16,164	—
4. National Investment Companies	975	—
5. Real Estate Financing & Development Companies	128	—
Sub-total, Private Initiative	46,747	11,237
Grand Total, all sectors	77,819	55,952

Source: Secretariat of Planning, Socialist People's Libyan Arab Jamahiriya. *The Economic and Social Transformation Plan* (1981-1985), Vol. I, pp. 76-77.

Table 3.8

Housing Construction and Shortages 1975-1980

1. No. of standard dwelling units in 1975	330,000
2. No. of housing units completed in 1976-80	77,819
3. No. of housing units that were replaced due to obsolescence during 1976-1980 (1 per cent annually of the 1975 housing stock)	16,500
4. No. of standard dwelling units in 1980	391,319
5. Estimated settled population in 1980	3,180,900
6. No. of settled families in 1980	531,035
7. Housing shortage in 1980	139,716

Note: Based on the world-wide average density of 1.2 families per standard housing unit, the housing needs in Libya would only be:

$$\frac{531{,}035}{1.2}$$

or 442,529 and the corresponding housing shortage would then be 51,210

Source: The Secretariat of Planning, Socialist People's Libyan Arab Jamahiriya, *The Economic and Social Transformation Plan* (1981-1985), Vol. I., p. 77.

declined, though the revolutionary principle of "Partners, Not Wage Workers" remained intact.

3.3d. **Health Services**

The achievement of economic and social justice in a society requires a provision for public health services. Public health services are not only essential for social justice in society, but also prerequisite for economic development since better physical and mental health of the workers enhances their capacity for work and production in the attainment of development targets. To this end, the Libyan Revolutionary Government adopted the following guidelines:

1. Implement the necessary organizational, administrative, and legislative measures which would ensure integration and coordination between the health services, on the one hand, and the other services and facilities which are complementary to them, on the other hand. These would include such services as nutrition, housing, environmental improvement, fresh water supply, sanitary sewage, and garbage disposal. This would also include the control of the centers which sell food and drinks to the public, as well as the provision of industrial safety services, etc.
2. Organize the health services and promote their efficient function accompanied by optimal norms, such as the number of doctors and the number of beds relative to the population.
3. Ensure the equitable distribution of both curative and preventive health services by giving priority to the remote areas which had been deprived in the past of such services.
4. Lay emphasis on preventive health programs, firstly, by undertaking to immunize all members of society against various diseases; secondly, by disseminating sound health and nutritional consciousness among all citizens, and, thirdly, by the development of control measures calculated to create a healthy environment, i.e., the prohibition of water and air pollution.
5. Strengthen and develop the health administration at various levels and to invest it with the necessary powers and authority which will enable it to discharge its responsibilities satisfactorily. Also, organize training programs to effect fur-

ther decentralization in the administration of health institutions and facilities.

6. Expand programs of scholarships for education and training abroad.

7. Take sufficient care of the health institutes and nursing schools in order to provide the necessary number of auxiliaries, health inspectors, staff nurses, assistants, and technicians in laboratories x-ray facilities, physical therapy, dental care, health education, and nutrition.

8. Give due attention to the dissemination of health culture and provide adequate guidance in health knowledge and practice.

9. Reinforce the health care services with necessary equipment and special mobile units which will enable it to reach remote areas inhabited by nomadic and semi-nomadic communities.

10. Undertake comprehensive research programs to assure better health care services for the whole society.

Based on these guidelines, the successive development plans of the Revolutionary Government paid special attention to the provision and development of health services.

Health services made great strides during the First Development Plan (1973-1975). Table 3.9 shows an increase in the number of beds, health centers, central dispensaries, general dispensaries, dental clinics, anti-TB centers, and mother and child care centers. In addition to the attention paid to the establishment of health institutions, efforts were also made to supply them with adequate manpower in order to improve the efficiency of services. Table 3.10 shows an increase in the number of physicians, pharmacists and chemists, nurses, technicians, and assistants.

Achievements of the First Development Plan (1973-1975) in the field of health training included sending abroad 469 doctors for specialization in the various branches of medicine: 90 doctors for higher studies and specialization, 33 pharmacists for specialization in the manufacturing and analysis of medicine, and 63 students to study dentistry. Also, a number of health technical and administrative personnel were sent abroad for training courses in the field of radiology, laboratories, nursing, medical apparatuses, artificial limbs, and hospital administration.

Table 3.9

Increase in Health Services During 1972-1975

Items	1972	1975	% Increase
No. of beds in hospitals	8,830	12,241	38.6
No. of health centers and central dispensaries	65	116	78.5
No. of general dispensaries	439	576	31.2
No. of dental clinics	58	70	20.7
No. of anti-TB centers	16	18	12.5
No. of mother and child care centers	71	93	31.0

Source: Secretariat of Planning, Socialist People's Libyan Arab Jamahiriya, *The Economic and Social Transformation Plan* (1976-1980), Part 2, p. 187.

Table 3.10

Increase in Manpower in the Health Sector During 1972-1975

Medical Staff	1972	1975	% Increase
Physicians	1,525	2,377	59.9
Pharmacists and Chemists	170	220	29.4
Nurses	4,315	7,987	85.1
Technicians and Assistants	857	1,296	51.2

Source: Secretariat of Planning, Socialist People's Libyan Arab Jamahiriya, *The Economic and Social Transformation Plan* (1976-1980), Part 2, p. 189.

The Second Development Plan (1976-1980) aimed at increasing the GDP of the health services sector from about L.D. 47.9 million in 1975 to about L.D. 84.4 million in 1980 (at constant 1975 prices) implying an annual compound growth rate of 12%. The actual data indicates that the GDP of this sector amounted to about L.D. 51.6 million in 1975; the estimate for 1980 was about L.D. 115 million which meant that the actual annual compound growth rate during 1976-1980 would be 17.4%. The increase in the growth of sectoral GDP is attributed to two main reasons, viz., rapid expansion of the health services which took place during the Plan and increased salaries of non-Libyan medical staff, as well as an increase in their number at a rate higher than that planned during the Second Development Plan, 1976-1980. The Gross Fixed Capital Formation, which at constant 1975 prices amounted to about L.D. 26.2 million in 1975, was estimated to reach about L.D. 65 million in 1980 or at an annual compound growth rate of 19.9%. The sectoral Gross Fixed Capital Formation was expected to reach about L.D. 214.7 million (in constant 1975 prices) during the development period 1976-1980. The current per capita expenditure on health services rose from L.D. 17.0 in 1975 to about L.D. 39.4 in 1980 or at a growth rate of 118.3%. This was in addition to the relevant share in the investments of the Transformation Plan for both the Health and Social Security sectors. Table 3.11 shows the GDP and the Gross Fixed Capital Formation at constant prices for 1975, as well as the allocations and expenditure of the budgets for 1975-1980.

The number of hospital beds increased from 10,080 in 1975 to 14,472 in 1980, at an annual compound growth rate of 7.5%. The hospital bed ratio per 1000 persons rose from 3.6 in 1975 to 4.5 beds in 1980. It should be noted that the Second Development Plan (1976-1980) aimed at increasing the number of hospital beds to about 21,024 or at a bed ratio of 6.5 per 1000 persons. The Basic Popular Congresses in 1978 and 1979 decided to build some additional health facilities so that the total number of hospital beds planned for 1980 would reach 25,009 or at a bed rate of 7.7 per 1000 persons. However, because of limited construction capacities, this target could not be reached. Table 3.12 shows the progress of health services from 1970 to 1980.

Table 3.11

Gross Domestic Product and Gross Capital Formation in the Health Sector, 1975-80

(In L.D. Million at 1975 Constant Prices)

			Development Budgets			
Year	Gross Domestic Product	Gross Fixed Capital Formation	Allo-cations	Expen-diture	Per-centage of Expenditure	Per Capita Current Expenditure
1975	51.6	26.2	26.2	20.9	78.6	17.0
1976	64.8	25.2	35.8	30.8	85.9	21.8
1977	79.0	35.5	47.1	39.7	84.4	24.8
1978	89.0	41.0	68.2	52.0	76.3	27.5
1979	101.1	50.0	69.1	66.0	95.5	29.7
1980						
(Planned)	115.0	65.0	90.0	85.0	94.4	39.4
(Anticipated)	184.4	—	—	—	—	—

Source: Secretariat of Planning, Socialist People's Libyan Arab Jamahiriya, *The Economic and Social Transformation Plan* (1981-1985), Vol. III, p. 2.

Table 3.12

Basic Health Services Indicators, 1970-1980

Particulars	1970	1975	1976	1977	1978	1979	1980 Expected	1980 Planned
No. of Hospital Beds	7,589	10,080	12,241	12,959	13,418	13,972	14,472	21,014
Bed rate per 1000 persons	3.4	3.8	4.3	4.4	4.5	4.5	4.5	6.5
No. of Polyclinics	11	12	12	28	28	28	28	28
No. of Health Centers	12	58	78	81	88 *	103	148	112
No. of T.B. Centers	9	18	19	19	22	22	22	28
Mother & Child Care Centers	48	96	99	108	112	127	172	99
No. of Laboratories	—	82	82	98	121	122	127	83

* 21 health centers were developed into rural hospitals with a capacity of 40-50 beds each.

Source: Secretariat of Planning Socialist People's Libyan Arab Jamahiriya, *The Economic and Social Transformation Plan* (1981-1985), Vol. III, p. 3.

With respect to medical manpower, the number of physicians rose from 2,779 in 1975 (one physician per 965 persons) to 4,390 in 1980 (one physician per 750 persons). The number of pharmacists and chemists increased from 528 in 1975 to about 990 in 1980 or at an annual growth rate of 11.7%.

The number of nursing staff increased from 9,388 in 1975 (one member of nursing staff per 285 persons) to about 13,500 in 1980 (one nursing personnel per 240 persons).

Similarly, the number of technicians and assistants increased from 1,335 in 1975 (one technician or assistant per 2000 persons) to about 2,300 in 1980 (one technician or assistant per 1400 persons). Table 3.13 shows the numbers and ratios of the medical and medical staff assistants from 1970 to 1980.

It seems fairly clear that the development of the public health sector within the socio-economic framework of Libya is remarkably successful. This success is reflected in the improvment of public health. The data regarding public health indicates that T.B. cases decreased from 0.50 per 1000 inhabitants in 1975 to about 0.29 per 1000 in 1980. The infant mortality per 1000 births decreased from 43.1 in 1975 to about 38 in 1980. The general mortality rate also declined from 7.4 per thousand inhabitants in 1975 to about 5.5 per 1000 in 1980.

3.3e. **Education**

Under the new socio-economic system of Libya, the educational and training policies are aimed at the creation of a generation which holds onto the faith and practice of Islam, but also is capable of undertaking the task of economic and social change and channelling it into the avenues that would lead to the creation of a progressive Libyan society. The preparation of expertise, propagation of technological and scientific advancement, formation of creative and innovative spirit, and procurement of technicians are some of the many targets set by the policy-makers throughout the 1970's.

During the First Development Plan (1973-1975) period, the educational sector witnessed remarkable development, extending to every stage and level of education. Table 3.14 shows the steady increase in the number of students, schools,

Table 3.13

Medical Staff 1970-1980

Description	1970	1975	1976	1977	1978	1979	1980
No. of physicians	783	2,779	3,116	3,183	3,627	4,110	4,390
No. of population per one physician	2,423	965	911	923	831	760	750
No. of pharmacists and chemists	91	528	610	698	738	862	990
No. of nursing staff	3,073	9,385	9,931	10,467	12,769	1,299	13,500
No. of population per number of nursing staff	585	286	286	281	236	240	240
No. of technicians and assistants	385	1,335	1,485	1,658	1,799	1,909	2,300
No. of population per technicians or asstt.	4,668	2,010	1,712	1,773	1,675	1,638	1,411
Estimated population (1,000)	1,797	2,683	2,839	2,939	3,014	3,127	3,245

Source: Secretariat of Planning, Socialist People's Libyan Arab Jamahiriya, *The Economic and Social Transformation Plan* (1981-85), Vol. III, p. 4.

Table 3.14

Development of the Number of Students (Boys and Girls), Schools, Classrooms and Teachers at the Various Level of General Education Throughout the Republic during the Period of the 1973/1975 Plan.

Education Level	Boys	Girls	Number of Students		Schools and Classrooms			Teachers		Class-room Density	Number of students per Teacher
			Total	Percentage Increase	Number Schools	Classrooms No.	Classrooms Percentage Increase	Number	Percentage Increase		
Elementary											
1972/1973	270,772	187,516	458,228		1,494	15,276		17,497		30.0	26.2
1975/1976	282,451	251,758	534,209	16.6	1,741	18,989	24.3	22,654	29.5	28.1	23.6
General Preparatory											
1972/1973	43,653	13,029	56,679		1,494	15,276		17,497		30.0	26.2
1975/1976	78,186	38,444	116,630	105.8	1,741	18,989	24.3	22,654	29.5	28.1	23.6
General Secondary											
1972/1973	8,126	1,976	10.902		43	385		974		28.3	11.2
1975/1976	13,276	3,563	16,839	54.6	66	633	64.4	1,720	76.6	26.8	9.8
Technical Secondary											
1972/1973	2,348	—	2,348		9	90		379		28.1	6.2
1975/1976	3,600	100	3,700	57.6	12	155	72.2	455	20.1	33.9	8.1
Teachers Institutes											
1972/1973	6,738	4,080	10,826		53	382		731		28.3	14.8
1975/1976	9,156	12,246	21,246	96.2	110	769	101.3	1,629	122.8	27.3	13.0

Source: Secretariat of Planning, Socialist People's Libyan Arab Jamahirya, *The Economic and Social Transformation Plan* (1976-1980); Part 2, p. 134.

classrooms, and teachers at various levels of general education in the period of the First Development Plan. Table 3.14 indicates that considerable increase in the number of female students contributed to the successful implementation priorities in the educational sector. It is particularly true in the case of the general preparatory educational level and at the Teacher's Training Institute where an increase in the number of female students from 1972/73 to 1975/76 was 295.1% and 297.4%, respectively.

Higher education was also given great importance during the First Plan Period. Measures were taken to increase the enrollment of university students. As a result, during this period the number of students in scientific and technological studies increased from 2,253 to 4,372, or by 94%; enrollment in the social sciences increased from 5,967 to 9,145 students, or by 53.5%. The increase in the number of students in the scientific areas can be attributed to the ever increasing facilities for such education in the Al-Fateh and Qar Younis Universities.

The Second Development Plan (1976-1980) was also successful in the educational sector. The number of students estimated to be enrolled in 1980-1981 was 1,025,200, as compared to 909,357 targeted in the plan, showing an implementation ratio of 113%. In terms of ratio to the population, it increased from 28.1% in 1975-1976 to 31.6% in 1980-1981. The annual growth rate of the total number of students during 1976-1980 was estimated at 6.3% as against 3.9% originally planned.

The significant development with regard to all levels of education is shown in Table 3.15. It indicates variations in the average annual growth rates in enrollment among different levels of education ranging from 3.5% in primary education to 20.1% in technical education. The differences between the planned and estimated annual growth rates of enrollment at various educational levels are also considerable: whereas in primary, preparatory and technical education, anticipated growth rates were higher than planned, they were lower in the case of general secondary and university and higher education.

The expansion of the educational system called for an increase in the number of classrooms at all levels. However, the increase from 27,066 in the school year 1975/1976 to

Table 3.15

Number of Students in Various Education Levels (1975/1976 - 1980/1981)

(in 1000)

Educational Level	1975/76 Actual	1979/80 Actual	1980-81		Annual Growth Rate 1975-1980	
			Anticipated	Planned	Anticipated	Planned
Primary Education	573.9	656.5	683.6	607.0	3.5	0.4
Preparatory Education	123.4	219.1	236.6	190.9	13.9	4.4
General Secondary Education	18.3	38.3	45.8	65.7	20.1	25.5
Technical Education	3.4	11.6	12.5	8.1	29.7	10.3
Teachers Training Institutes	21.1	31.2	27.4	12.2	5.4	-12.3
University and Higher Education	13.4	18.2	19.3	25.5	7.6	12.7
Total No. of Students	753.5	974.9	1,025.2	909.4	6.3	2.1
Ratio of the Students to the Population	28.1	31.2	31.6	28.0	—	—

Source: Secretariat of Planning, Socialist People's Libyan Arab Jamahiriya, *The Economic and Social Transformation Plan* (1981-1985), Vol. I, p. 86.

Table 3.16

Number and Density of the Classroom

Years	1975/1976		Expected		Planned	
Education	No. of class rooms	Class room density	No. of class rooms	Class room density	No. of class rooms	Class room density
Primary Education	21,521	26.7	25,990	26.3	33,593	18.1
Preparatory Education	3,980	31.0	7,784	30.4	9,464	20.2
General Secondary Education	649	28.1	1,478	31.0	2,189	30.0
Technical Secondary Education	133	25.5	460	27.1	300	27.2
Male and Female Teachers Institute	783	26.9	1,050	26.1	887	23.7
Total	27,066		36,857		46,433	

Source: Secretariat of Planning, Socialist People's Libyan Arab Jamahiriya, *The Economic and Social Transformation Plan* (1981-85), Vol. I, p. 88.

36,857 in the school year 1980/1981, was lower than the 46,433 classrooms envisaged in the Second Development Plan (1976-1980). Table 3.16 shows the number of classrooms and classroom density at the various educational levels during the preceding five-year plan period. The pace of building new classrooms during the period 1975/76-1980/81 could not cope with the rapid increase in the number of students at the various educational levels, with the result that with the exception of technical secondary education, the planned improvement in classroom density was not achieved.

The rapid expansion of the educational system called also for a sharp increase in the supply of teachers at all levels of education. There were 37,994 teachers in the school year 1975/1976, out of which 21,763 were Libyans (57.5% of the total). This number increased to 49,905 in the school year 1979/1980, out of which 36,946 were Libyans (74.0% of the total). These results are summarized in Table 3.17. It is important to note that the increase in the number of teachers resulted in reduction of the student/teacher ratio in Libyan schools.

The total number of students at the university and higher educational level rose from 13,418 in the school year 1975/1976 to 19,315 in 1980/1981, an increase of 43.4% which implies an annual compound growth rate of 7.6%. The increase in the number of girls was particularly rapid; it rose from about 2,359 in 1975/1976 to about 4,730 in 1980/1981, an increase of 102.6% and an annual compound growth rate of 15.2%. Another important aspect of the development of the educational sector is that the number of students enrolled in theoretical and practical studies rose sharply (see Table 3.18).

During the Second Development Plan (1976-1980), a number of new faculties and higher institutes were also being established. At Al-Fateh University, a Veterinary Medicine Faculty was set up in 1976/1977, and a Nuclear Energy Faculty in 1977/78. A faculty of Education at Sebha was established in 1976/1977. Moreover, three higher technological institutes were opened in 1976/1977, one for technology at Brak, one for electronics at Bani Walid, and one for mechanics and electricity at Hoon. In 1979/80, a higher administration and banking institute for women was also established. The results in

Table 3.17

Teachers by Sex and Nationality at Various Educational Levels in the School Year 1975/1976 and 1979/1980

	School Year 1975/1976						School Year 1979/1980					
	Libyans		Non Libyans		Total	Proportion of Libyans (Percent)	Libyans		Non Libyans		Total	Proportion of Libyans (Percent)
	Male	Female	Male	Female			Male	Female	Male	Female		
Compulsory Education Level												
Primary	12,798	4,856	6,075	2,429	26,158	67.5	15,387	12,072	2,545	485	30,489	90.0
Preparatory	3,124	363	3,602	765	7,854	44.4	6,064	2,002	4,543	1,094	13,703	58.8
Post Compulsory Education Level												
General Secondary	381	53	1,253	123	1,820	24.0	607	192	1,787	237	2,823	28.3
Technical Secondary	44	—	296	—	340	12.9	170	47	398	22	637	34.0
Male & Female Teachers Institute	181	63	1,214	374	1,832	13.3	287	118	1,304	444	2,153	18.8
Total	16,528	5,235	12,440	3,691	37,994	57.5	22,515	14,431	10,577	2,282	49,905	74

Source: Secretariat of Planning, Socialist People's Libian Arab Jamahiriya, *The Economic and Social Transformation Plan* (1981-1985), Vol. I, p. 89.

Table 3.18

The Number of Students Enrolled in Theoretical and Practical Studies

	Annual Compound Growth Rate During the Transformation Plan 1976-1980			Relative Distribution	
	Male	Female	Total	1975/76	1980/81
Theoretical Studies	1.2	12.6	3.7	67.9	56.4
Practical Studies	13.0	20.5	14.4	32.1	43.6
Total	5.6	15.2	7.6	100.0	100.0

Source: The Secretariat of Planning, Socialist People's Libyan Arab Jamahiriya, *The Economic and Social Transformation Plan*, (1981-85), Vol. I, p. 90.

the field of Education during the First and Second Development Plans in Libya suggest that a self-managed socio-economic system has a positive impact on the development of the educational sector in almost all dimensions. The most striking changes are the very big increases in the number of female students enrolled in every level from primary through university education. The main reason for the increase in the number of female students appears to be their new role as set by the developing socio-economic system.

3.4. Performance of the Libyan Experience

The ultimate purpose of our examining the development of economic and social sectors of Libya was to evaluate the development performance of the system in terms of simultaneous achievement of equity in distribution and efficiency in production, the criteria set by the Islamic economic system. Although we have discussed the developments and achievements of various economic and social sectors in detail, we have not determined whether or not the Libyan experience has, in fact, established equity in distribution and efficiency in production. This is the task of the following section.

3.4a. Equity

There are basically two methods to evaluate the reduction in economic inequality: first, in comparison to an international standard; second, in comparison to the planned objectives and targets within the economy. International comparisons of reduction in economic inequality are very difficult, both because of the poor quality of the data and because of the existence of numerous and different methods of measuring reduction in economic inequality. Thus, with a few exceptions, we shall mainly rely on the second method, namely, in comparison to the planned objectives and targets following some of the information presented in the previous section.

To pursue equitable distribution of income and wealth for the society, the Revolutionary Government of Libya combined the socialist pattern of income and wealth with the Islamic principle of economic justice. Elimination of private property incomes (socialist pattern), and income-sharing according to work performed by each member of the firm (principle of

Islamic economic justice) were considered the necessary conditions for equitable distribution of normal money incomes in Libya. Provision of housing, health, and educational services, combined with the equitable distribution of normal money incomes, were sufficient conditions to bring economic justice for the society.

The elimination of property incomes and the application of the principle of "Partners, Not Wage Workers" played an important role in the reduction of economic inequality. However, some differences in money income did exist among members of revolutionary committees, academicians, heads of higher educational institutions, head doctors, and higher officials of the General People's Congress. These differences were negligibly small and cannot be compared with the incomes of top party officials in other socialist states.[2]

As far as non-money incomes, such as imputed rent from owner-occupied dwellings, the subsidy element in state rents and free medical and educational services, Libya made a remarkable progress during the First and Second Development Plans to equalize the net advantages in incomes for everyone in the country.

The housing situation prior to the revolution was very bad both because of shortages and because of improper living conditions which existed for more than 53% of the occupants of the existing dwellings. According to the information available at the Housing Secretariat, there were only 300,000 units of livable places in 1969, despite the fact that there were only 365,000 families living in the country at that time. This means that there were 65,000 homeless families. During the First Development Plan (1973-1975) which preceded the revolution, the provision for housing to the homeless families was one of the most important objectives of the policy-makers. The public establishment for housing was asked to quickly construct dwellings to help solve this problem. The housing project was completed in 1974. Its units were distributed in the regions of Tripoli, Benghazi, Derna, and Sebha. Once the

[2]Matthews shows an elite group of 0.2% of the employed population with real income much above the average in Russia. M. Matthews, "Top incomes in the USSR: Towards a Definition of the Soviet Elite," *Survey,* 21 (1975), pp. 1-27.

immediate problem of the homeless families was solved, the state successfully implemented the policy based on equitable distribution of better housing facilities in order to reduce economic inequality.

An interesting example of equalization of non-money incomes among all members of the society is provided by the health sector. Unequal access to medical care, both as regards payments and quality, was a permanent feature of Libyan society prior to the present socio-economic system. Only about 5% of the urban population could afford to have complete medical facilities. In the rural areas, medical care had generally been scanty, of low quality, and had to be paid for. After the implementation of the present system, free medical care was introduced throughout the country. Under this system, health services, as measured by (estimated) mortality and morbidity statistics (see Table 3.19), were increased for all. The quality and access to care available to all urban and rural inhabitants were also improved according to the needs of respective localities.

Prior to the revolution, substantial income differences existed in Libya mainly due to the prevailing educational structure which offered uneven opportunities to the society. It was restricted to specific areas and to a few people who came from privileged families. Schooling was not free. Though fees were not high, yet they were not insignificant, particularly if there were several children in the family. Textbooks and stationery also had to be paid for, and there was an opportunity cost of schooling in terms of wages foregone. Furthermore, the better schools tended to charge more and took students almost exclusively from the rich and well-to-do families. The existence of these selective facilities, and the fact that only a small minority received education, caused massive economic inequalities in the society. But, after the revolution, the education became free of charge for everyone, from the elementary level to the university level. Accordingly, schools were built in remote and interior regions. The system made education obligatory and launched a plan to fight illiteracy in the society.

We can thus safely say that the economy of Libya under the new socio-economic system has performed remarkably well in reducing economic inequalities. Furthermore, if we

Table 3.19

Health Services in the Jamahiriya and Some Selected Countries

Countries	Birth rate per 1,000 inhabitants in 1977	Death rate per 1,000 inhabitants in 1977	Expected life at birth in 1977	Infant mortality rate per 1,000 births 1976	No. of population per one physician 1976
Oil Exporting countries					
Libya	48	14	55	55.7	1,020
Saudi Arabia	49	18	48	n/a	2,220
Kuwait	45	5	69	34.6 (1976)	850
Low Income countries					
Rowanda	51	19	46	50.4	39,350
Sudan	45	19	46	n/a	9,760
Kenya	51	14	53	51.4 (1973)	8,840
Middle Income countries					
Algeria	48	13	56	87.9 (1975)	5,590
Tunisia	32	12	57	52.1 (1974)	4,800
Syria	46	13	57	15.3 (1976)	2,510
Industrialized countries					
Sweden	12	12	75	8.0 (1977)	580
England	12	11	73	13.8 (1977)	670
Italy	13	10	73	20.9 (1975)	490
Centrally planned economies					
U.S.	18	9	70	27.7 (1974)	300
Poland	19	8	71	24.9 (1975)	620
Yugoslavia	18	9	69	35.2 (1977)	790

n/a = Not Available

Source: Secretariat of Planning, Socialist People's Libyan Arab Jamahiriya, *The Economic and Social Transformation Plan* (1976-1980), Vol. I, p. 99.

add to these quantitative results the consideration that the Libyans were developing their system by trial and error and were forced to change considerably the social and economic policies designed to reduce economic inequalities because they had no coherent experience or planning model to go by, then the total picture becomes more favorable. It is also important to recognize that the Libyan socio-economic system combined the Islamic principle of economic justice with the socialist pattern of equality. We believe that if the Libyan system had relied only on the principle of Islamic economic justice, the results would have been even more favorable.

3.4b. **Efficiency**

Inter-system comparisons of productivity and efficiency are as difficult as international comparisons of the distribution of income and wealth. Nevertheless, some work has been done in this area, notably by Bergson.

Bergson asserted two propositions: first, "that there is no evidence for the Marxist view that socialism is more efficient than capitalism" (Bergson, 1968), and, second, "that socialism . . . is markedly less efficient than capitalism" (Eckstein, 1971, p. 239). These conclusions are based on the data set out in Table 3.20 and 3.21. Table 3.20, column 2 shows that the dynamic efficiency of the Soviet economy, while better than that of the U.K. and the U.S.A., is worse than that of Italy, Germany, and France (First Proposition). Table 3.21, column 3 indicates that the static efficiency of the Soviet economy is worse than that of the U.S.A., France, Germany, and the U.K., but on a par with Italy (Second Proposition).[3] To be more specific, from Table 3.21, column 3, we observe that:

$$\frac{\Sigma P_{USA} X_{USA}}{(L,K)_{USA}} > \frac{\Sigma P_{USSR} X_{USSR}}{(L,K)_{USSR}} \qquad (1)$$

Now assume that each side of the inequality is a point on a production function with the following properties:

[3]By "dynamic efficiency" Bergson understands the rate of change of output per unit of inputs. By static efficiency he means output per unit of inputs at a given time.

Table 3.20

Relative Dynamic Efficiency (1950-1962)

	Average Annual Rate of Growth National Income Per Employed Worker (%)	Average Annual Rate of Growth of National Income Per Unit of Factor (Labor and Reproducible Capital) Inputs (%)
	(1)	(2)
United States	2.4	2.0
Northwest Europe	4.1	3.4
France	4.8	4.1
Germany	5.6	4.6
U.K.	1.9	1.4
Italy	5.3	4.7
U.S.S.R.	4.7	2.8

Source: A. Bergson, *Planning and Productivity under Soviet Socialism*, p. 53.

Table 3.21

Relative Static Efficiency in 1960 (U.S.A. = 100)

	National Income Per Employed Worker		National Income Per Unit of Factor (Labor and Reproducible Capital Factor) Inputs	
	Based on National Price Weights	Based on U.S. Price Weights	Based on National Price Weights	Based on U.S. Price Weights
	(1)	(2)	(3)	(4)
United States	100	100	100	100
Northwest Europe	44	56	50	63
France	43	55	49	62
Germany	43	55	52	63
U.K.	44	56	50	63
Italy	22	37	28	45
U.S.S.R.	22	38	28	45

Source: A. Bergson, *Planning and Productivity under Soviet Socialism*, p. 22.

a) Homogeneous labor and capital
b) Identical technology
c) Constant return to scale
d) The "System" is the only difference between the two economies.

Thus we can write:

$$Q_{USA} = f(K,L,T,S)_{USA} \tag{2}$$

$$Q_{USSR} = f(K,L,T,S)_{USSR} \tag{3}$$

Where Q is output, K is capital, L is labor, T is technology, and S is the system efficiency. We observe that:

$$\frac{Q_{USA}}{(L,K)_{USA}} > \frac{Q_{USSR}}{(L,K)_{USSR}} \tag{4}$$

$$\therefore S_{USA} > S_{USSR} \tag{5}$$

Since assumptions (a), (b), and (c) guarantee that L, K, and T are identical in both functions, then only differences in S can cause differences in Q/(L,K)

$$\therefore S_{CAPITALIST} > S_{SOCIALIST} \tag{6}$$

How much guidance, it is reasonable to ask, can we expect to get from Bergson's approach in analyzing efficiency in Libyan production? The answer, alas, is not very much. Bergson's work, in fact, only tests the neoclassical hypothesis, that is, the relationship between utilized inputs and the market value of output. He completely fails to test the Marxist hypothesis of the relationship between available inputs and the social utility of output.

It is also important to note that Bergson's conclusions are not necessarily valid if one or more of the four assumptions are false. For example, if assumption (b) is false and the U.S.A. used more advanced technology than the U.S.S.R., as much recent empirical work suggests, then it might be that the

Soviet system is more efficient than that of the U.S.A. Similarly, in view of assumption (d), let us take two countries, Czechoslovakia and India. Productivity level in Czechoslovakia is much higher than that in India. If we apply Bergson's method to them, we "observe" that capitalism, as exemplified by India, is markedly less efficient than socialism, as exemplified by Czechoslovakia; i.e., we observe a counter example to the static version of both Bergson inferences.

In light of the above discussion, it is fairly obvious that the Bergsonian approach of inter-system comparison of efficiency will not help us much in getting the clear picture of the efficiency of the Libyan experience. Therefore, the only alternative approach left at our disposal is to evaluate the efficiency of the Libyan experience in comparison to its own planned objectives and targets. The most straightforward and informative way to pursue this approach is to review the implementation ratios of some key targets during the latest Libyan development plan.

Table 3.22 shows the implementation ratios of 7 key targets of the Second Development Plan (1976-1980). The most successful implementation ratios of planned targets are related to the health and educational services where the implementation ratio concerning the number of physicians is estimated at 125%, and concerning the total number of students is estimated at 113%. However, disappointing results in implementing the planned targets can be seen in case of agricultural output (implementation ratio 37%), manufacturing output (implementation ratio 53%), and the number of completed housing units (implementation ratio 52%).

During the Second Development Plan period (1976-1980), the share of manufacturing in total GDP was planned to rise from 1.8% in 1975 to 4.8% in 1980, whereas the actual share was estimated at only 3.4%. The share of agriculture in total GDP, instead of increasing from 2.3% in 1975 to 2.6% in 1980, declined to 2.0%. Similarly, with regard to the efficiency of the development process in terms of productivity of capital, labor, and land, the prevailing picture is also highly unsatisfactory. Value added per person in such key productive activities as agriculture and manufacturing is very low. The low efficiency of investment in term of incremental capital/output ratio is extremely discouraging, particularly in the

Table 3.22

Estimated Implementation Ratios of the Key Targets of the Second Development Plan (L.D. In Million at 1975 Constant Prices)

Indicators	Planned	Anticipated Achievements	Implementation Ratio (%)
1. Total GDP*	6,692.2	5,058.0	76
2. GDP in Agriculture (1980)	174.4	99.0	57
3. GDP in Manufacturing (1980)	323.4	171.0	53
4. No. of Completed Housing Units (1976-1980)	150,000	77,800	52
5. No. of Physicians (1980)	3,450	4,300	125
6. No. of Hospital Beds (1980)	21,024	14,472	69
7. Total No. of Students (1980)	909,400	1,025,193	113

*Total GDP includes both GDP in oil and non-oil sectors.

Source: Secretariat of Planning, Socialist People's Libyan Arab Jamahiriya, *The Economic and Social Transformation Plan* (1981-1985), Vol. I, p. 6.

agricultural sector where the actual estimated investment of L.D. 942 million during 1976-1980 results in an additional output of only L.D. 16 million. In the Second Development Plan, it was assumed that the investment of L.D. 942 million would at least generate an additional output of L.D. 90 million. On the basis of such observations, it appears that although the new socio-economic system of Libya did play an important role in the reduction of economic inequalities, it could not resolve the problem of efficiency in production. Due to immense inefficiencies in key sectors, such as agriculture and manufacturing, the fundamental structural problems facing the economy remained the same. Dependence on the petroleum sector is still very high; reliance on expatriate labor is heavy; and the share of imports in total supply of foodstuffs and industrial consumer goods is very large.

3.5. **Conclusions and Summary**

The data presented in this chapter shows that the Libyan self-management system as a solution for simultaneous achievement of equality and efficiency is, at best, incomplete. The main reason, as mentioned earlier, is that the system lays its foundations on two mutually exclusive frameworks, namely, Islam and socialism. Although the Libyan model follows the second and third basic characteristics of the Islamic economic framework, it substitutes public ownership for dual ownership, the first and the most fundamental characteristic of the Islamic economic system. It is important to note that problems of equity and efficiency do not disappear if we simply apply the principle of "Partners, Not Wage Workers" and completely ignore the concept of dual ownership. It is also important to note that equity and efficiency objectives can only be achieved if all basic characteristics of the Islamic economic framework are put into practice. By introducing in some sense self-management in capitalism or socialism, one is not reproducing the Islamic work motivation which is necessary for economic efficiency. In other words, a system that possesses the "participation in management" condition with different ownership relations and different interests in the proceeds of the firms' outputs is likely to have different motivational properties. Thus, a system of absolute ownership plus rules of self-management will not yield the same results as system in which all characteristics of the Islamic economic system are taken into account.

Bibliography

Alchian, A., and H. Demsetz. "Production, Information Costs and Economic Organization," *American Economic Review,* 62 (1972), pp. 777-795.

Arrow, K. J. "A Difficulty in the Concept of Social Welfare," *Journal of Political Economy,* 58 (1950), pp. 328-346.

Arrow, K. J. *Social Choice and Individual Values,* 2nd ed. New York: Wiley, 1963.

Arrow, K. J. "Uncertainty and the Welfare Economics of Medical Care," *American Economic Review,* 53 (1963), pp. 941-973.

Arrow, K. J. "Some Ordinalist-Utilitarian Notes on Rawls's Theory of Justice," *Journal of Philosophy,* 70 (1973), pp. 245-263.

Arrow, K. J., and F. H. Hahn. *General Competitive Analysis.* San Francisco: Holden-Day, 1971.

Atkinson, A. B. "On the Measurement of Inequality," *Journal of Economic Theory,* 2 (1970), pp. 244-263.

Awan, A. A. "Equality, Efficiency, and Work Incentive in a Global Economy," Mimeographed, 1981.

Bator, F. M. "The Simple Analytics of Welfare Maximization," *American Economic Review,* 47 (1957), pp. 22-59.

Bator, F. M. "Convexity, Efficiency and Markets," *Journal of Political Economy,* 69 (1961), pp. 480-483.

Baumol, W. J. *Welfare Economics and the Theory of the State.* Cambridge, Mass.: Harvard University Press, 1952.

Bentham, J. *An Introduction to the Principles of Morals and Legislation.* 1789.

Bentzel, R. "The Social Significance of Income Distribution Statistics," *Review of Income and Wealth,* 16 (1970), pp. 253-264.

Bergson, A. "A Reformulation of Certain Aspects of Welfare Economics," *Quarterly Journal of Economics,* 52 (1938), pp. 310-334.

Bergson, A. *The Economics of Soviet Planning.* New Haven: Yale University Press, 1964.

Bergson, A. *Essays in Normative Economics.* Cambridge, Mass.: Harvard University Press, 1966.

Bergson, A. *Planning and Productivity under Soviet Socialism.* New York: Columbia University Press, 1968.

Béteille, A. *Social Inequality.* Harmondsworth: Penguin, 1969.

Breit, W., and W. P. Culbertson, Jr. "Distributional Equality and Aggregate Utility: Comment," *American Economic Review,* 60 (1970), pp. 435-441.

Buchanan, J. M. "A Hobbesian Interpretation of the Rawlsian Difference Principle," *Kyklos,* 29 (1976), pp. 5-25.

Bury, J. B. *The Idea of Progress.* New York: Dover, 1932.

Champernowne, D. "The Graduation of Income Distribution," *Econometrica,* 20 (1952), pp. 591-615.

Champernowne, D. "A Model of Income Distribution," *Economic Journal,* 63 (1953), pp. 318-351.

Condorcet, M. J. A. N. C. de. *Sketch of a Historical Picture of the Progress of the Human Mind.* 1795.

Crozier, M. *The Bureaucratic Phenomenon.* Chicago: University of Chicago Press, 1964.

Cyert, R. M., and J. G. March (eds.). *A Behavioral Theory of the Firm.* Englewood Cliffs, N.J.: Prentice-Hall, 1963.

Dasgupta, P. "On Some Problems Arising from Professor Rawls' Conception of Distributive Justice," *Theory and Decision,* 4 (1974), pp. 325-344.

Debreu, G. *The Theory of Value.* New York: Wiley, 1959.

Diamond, P. A. "Cardinal Welfare, Individualistic Ethics, and Interpersonal Comparisons of Utility: A Comment," *Journal of Political Economy,* 75 (1967), pp. 765-766.

Dobb, M. H. *Welfare Economics and the Economics of Socialism.* Cambridge, England: Cambridge University Press, 1969.

Domar, E. "The Soviet Collective Farm as a Producer Cooperative," *American Economic Review,* 56 (1966), pp. 734-757.

Dorfman, R., P. A. Samuelson, and R. M. Solow. *Linear Programming and Economic Analysis.* New York: McGraw-Hill, 1958.

Eckstein, A. *Comparison of Economic Systems.* Berkeley: University of California Press, 1971.

Ellman, M. *Soviet Planning Today.* Cambridge, England: Cambridge University Press, 1971.

Fisher, F. M., and J. Rothenberg. "How Income Ought to be Distributed: Paradox Lost," *Journal of Political Economy,* 69 (1961), pp. 162-180.

Fisher, F. M., and J. Rothenberg. "How Income Ought to be Distributed: Paradox Enow," *Journal of Political Economy,* 70 (1962), pp. 88-93.

Furubotn, E. G. "Toward a Dynamic Model of the Yugoslav Firm," *Canadian Journal of Economics,* 4 (1971), pp. 182-197.

Girvetz, H. K. *The Evolution of Liberalism.* New York: Collier, 1963.

Godwin, W. *Enquiry Concerning Political Justice.* 1798.

Gordon, S. "The New Contractarians," *Journal of Political Economy,* 84 (1976), pp. 573-590.

Gorman, W. M. "Community Preference Fields," *Econometrica,* 21 (1953), pp. 63-80.

Gorman, W. M. "The Structure of Utility Functions," *Review of Economic Studies,* 35 (1968a), pp. 367-389.

Gorman, W. M. "Duality and Separability," Department of Political Economy, lectures at The Johns Hopkins University, 1980.

Graaff, J. de V. *Theoretical Welfare Economics.* Cambridge, England: Cambridge University Press, 1957.

Gray, A. *The Socialist Tradition.* London: Longmans, 1963.

Hardy, G., J. Littlewood, and G. Polya. *Inequalities.* Cambridge, England: Cambridge University Press, 1934.

Harrod, R. F. "Another Fundamental Objection to Laissez-Faire," *Economic Journal,* 46 (1936), pp. 163-168.

Harsanyi, J. C. "Cardinal Welfare, Individualistic Ethics, and Interpersonal Comparisons of Utility," *Journal of Political Economy,* 63 (1955), pp. 309-321.

Hayek, F. A. *The Constitution of Liberty.* South Bend, Indiana: Gateway, 1960.

Hicks, J. R. "The Foundations of Welfare Economics," *Economic Journal,* 49 (1939), pp. 696-712.

Hobbes, T. *Leviathan.* 1651.

Holesovsky, V. "Planning Reforms in Czechoslovakia," *Soviet Studies,* 19 (1968), pp. 544-556.

Huberman, L., and P. M. Sweezy. *Socialism in Cuba.* New York: Monthly Review Press, 1969.

ibn Khaldūn, Abd al-Rehmān. *Muquddimah.* Cairo: al-Maktabah al-Tijāriyyah al-Kubrā, n.d.

Iqbal, Muhammad. *The Reconstruction of Religious Thought in Islam.* Lahore: Shaikh Muhammad Ashraf, 1954.

Kaldor, N. "Welfare Propositions and Interpersonal Comparisons of Utility," *Economic Journal,* 49 (1939), pp. 549-552.

Kant, I. *Grundlegung zur Metaphysik der Sitten.* 1785. English translation by T. K. Abbott, *Fundamental Principles of the Metaphysics of Ethics.* London: Longmans, 1907.

Kant, I. *Kant's Political Writings.* H. Reiss (ed.), Cambridge, England: Cambridge University Press, 1970.

Katsenelinboigen, A. "Coloured Markets in the Soviet Union," *Soviet Studies,* 29 (1977a), pp. 62-85.

Katsenelinboigen, A., and H. S. Levine. "The Soviet Case," *American Economic Review* Papers and Proceedings, 67 (1977), pp. 61-66.

Koopmans, T. C. *Three Essays on the State of Economic Science.* New York: McGraw-Hill, 1957.

Krupp, S. R. "Equilibrium Theory in Economics and in Functional Analysis as Types of Explanation," in *Functionalism in the Social Sciences.* Philadelphia: American Academy of Political and Social Science, 1965.

Lange, O. "On the Economic Theory of Socialism," *Review of Economic Studies,* 4 (1936), pp. 53-71.
Lange, O. "The Foundations of Welfare Economics," *Econometrica,* 10 (1942), pp. 215-228.
Lange, O. *Political Economy.* London: Pergamon Press, 1963.
Lerner, A. P. *The Economics of Control.* London: MacMillan, 1944.
Little, I. M. D. "Social Choice and Individual Values," *Journal of Political Economy,* 60 (1952), pp. 422-432.
Levhari, D., Y. Oron, and D. Pines. "A Note on Unequal Treatment of Equals in an Urban Setting," *Journal of Urban Economics,* 5 (1978), pp. 278-284.
Loevinsohn, E. "Liberty and the Redistribution of Property," *Philosophy and Public Affairs,* 6 (1977), pp. 226-239.
Mandel, E. *Marxist Economic Theory.* Translated by B. Pearce. New York: Monthly Review Press, 1969.
Marshall, A. *Principles of Economics.* London: MacMillan, 1980.
Marx, K. *Capital.* 1867.
Marx, K. *Critique of the Gotha Programme.* 1875.
Matthews, M. "Top Incomes in the USSR: Towards a Definition of the Soviet Elite," *Survey,* 21 (1975), pp. 1-27.
Meade, J. *Efficiency, Equity and the Ownership of Property.* Cambridge, Mass.: Harvard University Press, 1965.
Mill, J. S. *On Liberty.* 1859.
Mirrlees, J. A. "The Optimum Town," *Swedish Journal of Economics,* 74 (1972), pp. 114-135.
Newberry, D. M. G. "A Theorem on the Measurement of Inequality," *Journal of Economic Theory,* 2 (1970), pp. 264-266.
Nove, A. *The Soviet Economy:* An Introduction. New York: Praeger, 1961.
Nozick, R. *Anarchy, State and Utopia.* New York: Basic Books, 1974.
Pateman, C. *Participation and Democratic Theory.* Cambridge, England: Cambridge University Press, 1970.
Papageorgiou, G. J. "Social Values and Social Justice," *Economic Geography,* 56 (1980), pp. 110-119.
Pareto, V. *Cours d'Économie Politique.* Lausanne: Rouge, 1897.

Pareto, V. *Manuale di Economia Politica.* Milan: Societa Editrice Libraria, 1897.

Pigou, A. C. *Wealth and Welfare.* London: MacMillan, 1912.

Pigou, A. C. *The Economics of Welfare.* London: MacMillan, 1920.

Rawls, J. *A Theory of Justice.* Cambridge, Mass.: Harvard University Press, 1971.

Rawls, J. "Some Reasons for the Maximin Principle," *American Economic Review,* 64 (1974), pp. 141-146.

Robbins, L. *An Essay on the Nature and Significance of Economic Science.* London: Allen & Unwin, 1932.

Robbins, L. "Interpersonal Comparisons of Utility," *Economic Journal,* 48 (1938), pp. 635-641.

Robertson, D. H. *Utility and All That.* London: Allen & Unwin, 1952.

Robinson, J. "The Soviet Collective Farm as a Producer Cooperative: Comment," *American Economic Review,* 57 (1967), pp. 222-223.

Rousseau, J. J. *Social Contract and Discourses.* 1755.

Runciman, W. G., and A. K. Sen. "Games, Justice and the General Will," *Mind,* 74 (1965), pp. 554-562.

Runciman, W. G. *Relative Deprivation and Social Justice.* London: Routledge, 1966.

Samuelson, P. A. *Foundations of Economic Analysis.* Cambridge, Mass.: Harvard University Press, 1947.

Samuelson, P. A. "The Evaluation of Real National Income," *Oxford Economic Papers,* 2 (1950), pp. 1-27.

Saint-Pierre, A. F. C. de. *Observations on the Continuous Progress of Universal Reason.* 1737.

Saposnik, S. "Power, the Economic Environment and Social Choice," *Econometrica,* 42 (1974), pp. 461-470.

Scitovsky, T. "A Note on Welfare Propositions in Economics," *Review of Economic Studies,* 9 (1941), pp. 77-88.

Secretariat of Planning, Socialist People's Libyan Arab Jamahiriya, *The Economic and Social Transformation Plan* (1976-1980), Part 2.

Secretariat of Planning, Socialist People's Libyan Arab Jamahiriya, *The Economic and Social Transformation Plan* (1981-1985), Vol. I and Vol. III.

Sen, A. K. "Labour Allocation in a Cooperative Enterprise," *Review of Economic Studies,* 33 (1966), pp. 361-371.

Sen, A. K. *On Economic Inequality.* Oxford: Clarendon Press, 1973.

Stone, K. "The Origins of Job Structures within the Steel Industry," *Review of Radical Political Economics,* VI (1973), pp. 113-173.

Qadhafi, M. *The Green Book.* Tripoli: Secretariat of Information, 1976.

Tinbergen, J. "A Positive and a Normative Theory of Income Distribution," *Review of Income and Wealth,* 16 (1970), pp. 221-234.

Tobin, J. "On Limiting the Domain of Inequality," *Journal of Law and Economics,* 13 (1970), pp. 263-278.

Vanek, J. *The General Theory of Labor-Managed Market Economies.* Ithaca: Cornell University Press, 1970.

Vanek, J. "Some Fundamental Considerations on Financing and the Form of Ownership Under Labor Management," in *Economic Structure and Development: Essays in Honour of Jan Tinbergen.* Amsterdam: North-Holland Publishing Company, 1973.

Ward, B. "The Firm in Illyria: Market Syndicalism," *American Economic Review,* 48 (1958), pp. 556-589.

Wood, A. W. "The Marxian Critique of Justice," *Philosophy and Public Affairs,* 1 (1972), pp. 244-282.

Index of Names

Subject Index